MAKING THE MOST OF
SMALL GARDENS

MAKING THE MOST OF
SMALL GARDENS

GREEN OASES IN SMALL SPACES

© Naumann & Göbel Verlagsgesellschaft mbH, a subsidiary of
VEMAG Verlags- und Medien Aktiengesellschaft, Cologne
www.apollo-intermedia.de

Complete production: Naumann & Göbel Verlagsgesellschaft mbH, Cologne
Printed in Poland

ISBN 3-625-10756-2

Contents

THE MAIN GARDEN   10

THE FRONT GARDEN   18

ROCK GARDENS 36

VEGETABLE GARDENS 74

ORNAMENTAL GARDENS 88

PLANTS FOR SMALL GARDENS   114

TENDING THE GARDEN   144

INDEX   158

INTRODUCTION

"Imagination creates its own space". This more or less sums up the special challenges faced by anyone designing a small garden. The restrictions may make many things impossible, but that doesn't mean the garden has to be boring. On the contrary, lack of space can be a spur to your inventive talents, and your garden can become a small gem.

Wide is the world and fair, but o, how I thank Heaven that I have a garden, confined, dainty, that belongs to me alone. (Johann Wolfgang von Goethe)

Anyone who has visited the carefully restored garden behind Goethe's house in Weimar, Germany will know what the poet meant with his joyful exclamation: the most important tasks are those close at hand, and people who are constantly dreaming of far fields often don't see what is under their noses, and fail to recognize that limitations can create opportunities as well.

True, Goethe's garden is no suburban "pocket handkerchief". But we are not concerned here about a few square metres more or less, but with making the most of what is available. However small your plot of land may be, it offers plenty of room for creative gardening—provided you keep its size in mind. For making the most of your garden does not mean cluttering it up. On the contrary, your aim should be to create a feeling of expansiveness where there is none by means of clever design and sense of line.

This book aims to give you ideas on how to do this, as well as more general gardening tips. A garden's size—or, in this case, lack of it—does not affect the basic rules about sowing, upkeep and harvesting. It is simply all done on a small scale, allowing you to concentrate much more on detail than you could with a park-sized garden. Here, every shrub counts, every tree has its individual importance, and lettuce or vegetables from your own raised bed become a delicacy.

And that is what this book is all about: the close relationship that you can establish with a small piece of land. Whether the purpose of your garden is to acquaint your children with natural processes, to get some exercise after a stressful day's work, or simply to create a natural space of peace and tranquillity—there is nowhere you will feel more at home than, as Goethe puts it, in your "confined, dainty little garden".

THE
MAIN GARDEN

ORNAMENTAL AND KITCHEN GARDEN IN ONE

Of course, you can design your small garden solely as an ornamental garden, a lawn or a kitchen garden. But these examples show that you have several options even where space is limited. And if you take an inquisitive look at successful gardens in your neighbourhood, you will see that certain combinations have a charm all their own.

> A small garden means a lot of decision-making. Early on comes the question: to enclose or not to enclose? Here is a nice compromise: a wooden fence softened in effect by an ensemble of shrubs and bright flowers.

If you haven't much space, you have to make up for it with planning. This is a basic rule when designing small garden paradises. It doesn't mean you can't be spontaneous, but it is a reminder that planting trees or large shrubs, for example, has very long-lasting consequences. They can impose unwanted restrictions if you haven't thought about what is to flower and grow around them, under them, in front and behind them. The questions start with the garden enclosure or even with the question of whether an enclosure is necessary or useful at all: a fence or a hedge or just open?

This is only intended as a small warning to make you pause before, armed with your tools, you resolutely head off for your new garden and go into action. Now, let's take things step by step. The first question is, what are your expectations of your little piece of earth? Recreation, flowery splendor, bountiful harvests, room for play and activity? You are not likely to have just one of these in mind, but a mixture—and that mixture has to be the right one.

To help you make up your mind, we recommend that you steal. Yes, you have read right, but possibly misunderstood! What we mean is stealing with your eyes; in other words, looking at successful solutions or, to be more precise, solutions that accord particularly well to your personal ideas.

You will certainly never find a perfect model, as conditions—the shape of the piece of land, the type of soil, the light, etc.—always vary somewhat. But these vary the least in your immediate neighborhood, which is why your neighbors' advice and longer experience with the location can be an invaluable source of information. After all, you can see at first glance whether the neighbors know what they are about. And if they have created something similar to what you have in mind, a conversation over the garden fence might pave the way for a beneficial relationship. Nothing unites people more than common interests, although there's always bound to be a tiny bit of competition, of course. You'll soon notice yourself: in time, gardeners often develop a certain artistic vanity.

Or, if they have concentrated on planting vegetables, gardeners compete for the best harvest. Of course any competitive feelings pale beside the positive effects working and living outdoors can have on health and well-being. In beginning to turn your piece of the outdoors into a useful and pleasant place, you will experience how spiritually fulfilling and physically refreshing it is to live and work in a garden, particularly in today's busy world.

If your garden is to be mainly for rest and recreation, some form of seating is a good idea. Surrounding greenery will make it even more inviting.

Even where there is not much room, ornamental plants and vegetables can be combined to create a relaxed and pretty effect.

PLANNING THE GARDEN

Wherever you start gardening, you will generally find some elements already there and include them in your plans. Take photographs of your plot and make time to consider what your garden is to look like. Its small dimensions make a certain amount of planning necessary, although you don't have to measure everything down to the last degree.

You won't be needing many paths in a small garden, but the few there are will be structurally all the more important. For this reason, they lend themselves well to being edged with vegetation. If you have just one central path in a long, narrow garden, with all the beds and plants accessible from it or only a few dead-end paths going off to the sides, it is often a good idea to give it the status of a "main thoroughfare". Putting in flower beds along both sides can give this effect. Mini avenues with shrubs, herbaceous perennials or slender conifers can also emphasise a central path.

If you find this too monotonous or "square" you can widen the path in places, perhaps decorating the little "bays" you have formed with circular flower beds or colourful tubs of

Often there is only room for one path through your little idyll. You can turn it into a splendid avenue by putting in flower beds on both sides flanked by a row of medium-height rose bushes.

Colourful annual flowers like the sunflower are a real delight—but when designing your garden, remember to provide decoration for the cooler seasons as well.

flowers. These can be changed and moved as desired, and are a wonderful means of making small gardens more interesting. Putting in circular patches of lawn in the bays also provides a nice emphasis. Changing the level of the ground or using different levels that already exist will give you the opportunity to put in small sets of steps. The steps may be made of brick or natural stone, and have plants bordering them and growing out of any gaps and joints.

In the last section, we briefly mentioned the border to neighbouring properties. Happily, in new town house developments, fences are now often dispensed with. But sometimes you may want to emphasise your garden's individuality. In this case, use a low hedge, a raised bed or perhaps the edge of a lawn instead of a fence or a wall. However, if walls already exist, climbing plants can soften the appearance of the bare stone. Of course, you won't want to do without annual flowering plants or spring and summer flowers. But we would advise you to think of the more inhospitable seasons as well and not to use up all the area available. Without evergreen conifers like junipers or dwarf balsam firs to

decorate them, small gardens in particular tend to look rather dreary when days become bleaker. After all, green is said to be the colour of hope.

And one other thing to remember: you'll be wanting to live in your garden as well. Set up benches here and there, and make yourself cosy corners or pergolas to sit in. If you have a little more room, you might even build a small summerhouse. It can have a corner or separate room in which to store garden equipment, or it can even be covered with greenery like an enchanted castle so that the children can use it to play at fairy tales.

A colourful circular flower bed with flowering and evergreen plants can break up the monotony of a patch of lawn.

GREENING PATIOS, BALCONIES AND ROOFS

Even if you barely have any exterior space you can still garden. On your patio, on your balcony or even on your roof, there's always space for greenery. If you don't have enough horizontal space, go vertical. Or you can make your patch of ground into a water garden.

Climbing plants are the first and best choice for "upright" gardens. They are easy to shape and can be guided wherever you want using supports. Their thick foliage and abundant blossoms give you depth as well as height. You can cultivate climbing plants in tubs or troughs and use them, for example, to create a screen or a green windbreak by letting them grow up a frame of the required breadth. Climbers will also make sheds, carports and other unsightly items more attractive, softening their contours and brightening them up. And when in bloom, some climbing plants create an almost exotic atmosphere with their fragrance and colour. They can turn a balcony into a summerhouse, an entrance into a triumphal arch.

If you choose a good mix of plants, you will reap their benefits almost all year round. Some of these plants can be recommended even for winter, such as evergreen clematis or winter jasmine. And vegetable gardeners can also indulge their predilection, for instance, by

A water garden always generates a very special atmosphere. The stone border around the water's edge can be softened somewhat by a varied composition of flowering pot plants and a cushion of ground covering plants.

growing tomatoes in pots—said to be a good protection against mosquitoes—or by covering the walls of their houses with vines. If the summer is a good one and the location is sunny and protected, grapes can be harvested and eaten even in more northerly regions.

Water features in a garden—and a true water garden even more—create a very special atmosphere. This does require more than just a patio, and roofs cannot be used for structural and safety reasons. If you have a very small plot of land or the garden is very close to the house, you will feel some of the refreshing effect inside as well. You may feel the mosquitoes, too, if you don't take preventive action: fish and sala-manders are reliable larvae killers.

In general, the ebb and flow of the seasons of the year play a less and less important role in modern life. Gardeners have an advantage here, too, as they remain connected to the rhythm of nature, which governs the lives of humans just as much as it does that of plants, whether we are aware of it or not. Gardeners know, for example, that they have to keep winter in mind when planning flower beds and planting shrubs. They will put in evergreen plants to provide foliage when others plants have lost theirs, and make sure the garden contains vertical elements, as described at the start of this section, to add pleasing structure. Trees and shrubs, frames for climbing plants and archways in fences provide decorative highlights even in the cold and snow.

Necessity is the mother of invention: even on bal-conies and roofs, fans of abundant greenery can indulge their passion (opposite page).

White idyll: evergreen plants and vertical ele-ments like this arched gateway give pleasure to the eye in winter as well.

The Front
Garden

AN INVITING FRONT GARDEN

Normally, there is little room for gardening creativity in front of a house. For starters, the front of a house often faces north or northeast. This means that there is not much sunlight and only certain plants will thrive there. And then, most house owners want to make the most of the southern side, which is why the patio and the main garden are most often situated there.

Visitors immediately feel welcome if the area in front of your house is green and inviting. The front garden serves as a "calling card" for your home.

However, the front garden should under no circumstances be neglected, because it gives everyone approaching your home their first impression, and will determine how welcome visitors to your home feel. The kind of front garden you have says a lot about you, your preferences and your taste.

Plain lawns look unimaginative or even perfunctory, and it would be even more unappealing to cover the area in front of the house with some sort of paving. A few containers of bright flowers or some climbing plants to soften walls or fences give things a much more friendly and inviting impression.

(not too large), creeping juniper, St. Johnswort and ivy, although some people associate the latter with unpleasant memories of cemeteries. You must keep in mind the final height of any trees and shrubs, because you could make the shady side of the house look even shadier and cause the front rooms to be darker than necessary. As an eye-catcher, it can be enough to surround the front gate with a hedge or put a slender, relatively tall plant next to the front door, such as a laurel tree in a tub or a mahonia. This shrub's waxy, evergreen leaves are very pretty and give off a pleasant fragrance in spring. Daphnes can also lend the entrance a positive atmosphere. Honeysuckle climbing on a wall is also a lovely "green greeting".

A green oasis in front of the house: the dense greenery provides a screen for the entrance.

It is possible to have plenty of variety even in a front garden. The plants used here recall the atmosphere of a heath; they are also easy to care for.

And if you make the best of things by using the little space and sunlight available to create a green and flowering oasis, your visitors are sure to feel more welcome straightaway.

You may not always manage to make your front garden look as luxuriant as the three examples we show here, but it does not have to be boring. Evergreen trees or shrubs planted alongside paths or outbuildings like garages and carports will give the garden some colour even in winter and provide a friendly touch. Here are a few tips: cherry laurel, European privet, cotoneasters, some viburnums, epimediums and Algerian ivy all have attractive blossoms and many of them bear colourful berries right up into spring. Conifers are an obvious addition, but of course only those that don't grow too large, otherwise after a time you won't be able to see your house for the trees. Conifers will also give your front garden some contour in winter.

We would advise you to put in ground-covering plants instead of lawn, which, when you don't have much space available, looks rather unimaginative and what's more, is hard to mow. Plants that may be used as ground cover include representatives from the erica family, ranging from heather to rhododendrons

GREENERY FOR PAVED AREAS AND WALLS

A front garden has to accommodate a number of items: bicycles, garbage bins, parking, etc. Quite a lot of it will often need to be paved in addition to any paths. Placing large pots with flowers or green plants here and there will stop it from looking dull. Vertical stone surfaces can be decorated with hanging flowerpots and creepers.

Pots with green or flowering plants are an attractive feature in any front garden. They are excellent decoration for paved or tiled surfaces and can easily be moved to another location when desired.

Vertical surfaces also include the garden fence, which acts as a border as well as offering some protection. The front fence is often on top of a low wall that is interrupted by the front gate. It is almost always a good idea to cover it with greenery. Evergreen plants are best, as they stop the pales or bars from looking too severe in winter. If the fence is directly in the ground, it easily can be replaced or supplemented by a hedge. Hedges are preferable in most cases, as they provide valuable shelter for small animals and birds. What is more, they give better protection than fences against street noise and dust. Recommended hedge plants are:

- Fast growing cypresses
- Easily pruned privet
- Cherry laurel, with its glossy foliage
- Holly or barberry, both very prickly
- Yew, which provides dense shelter
- European hornbeam, which retains its foliage in winter, albeit brown and not green
- Firethorn, which makes a tapestry-like effect

In shady areas, green and evergreen plants and shrubs can also flourish behind a fence or hedge. Plantain lilies, ferns and moss, as well as "carpets" of angel's tears, patches of dead nettles, tufts of grass and attractively pruned box create an "emerald" garden. Shaped shrubs complete the ensemble. The delicate pink fruits of prickly heath will provide you with colour in autumn, while heather, dogwood and the yellow edges of the leaves of the spindle tree will brighten up the green. The blue blossoms of speedwell will give the foliage a darker tint.

Although it is very important to prepare for winter, you should also make use of each season's strong points. If there is room for

flowerbeds, annual plants and bulb flowers brighten up a garden marvellously in spring and summer. They can also be planted in troughs, pots and hanging flowerpots. This means they can occasionally be moved to various positions as eyecatchers—but not too often! Useful plants like herbs can also contribute greatly to a front garden, as they provide fragrance in addition to their flowers.

The garbage bin, which is often kept in the front garden for convenience, is likely the most disturbing item there. It can be concealed well behind plants, but you can also obtain various artificial enclosures for it. One quick solution is to use hollow cement bricks with different geometrical patterns to build a square wall, which can be covered with creepers. The openings in the bricks give the plants support and create an interesting combination of stone and foliage.

If the area in front of your house is too small for a garden, climbing plants are an ideal alternative for making the entrance green and friendly.

Colourful flowers please the eye not only in the garden, but also in front of a house. Pots and troughs of terracotta or stone can be placed on steps or around the front door.

THE PATH TO YOUR FRONT DOOR

Do you want to emphasise the path to your house, or make it look more casual? Like so many things, this is a matter of taste. A straight path of neatly laid paving stones or bricks can be very attractive, as can one made of gravel or natural stone that approaches the entrance from the side, at an angle, or in a winding fashion. Cement or asphalt are not as advisable.

There is no reason a short, straight path has to be boring. With some imagination, you can find very unique solutions, like this romantic arch covered in climbing roses, which accentuates the shape of the front door.

The route your path takes will also depend on the distance to be covered from the front gate. If it is only a matter of a few metres a winding path would be rather silly. If the front gate is to the side of the house, however, a slight curve to give a front-on approach to the house is more possible. If the distance is longer and there is a double set of steps leading to the front door, you could think about having a fork in the path or making it go around a semi-circular flowerbed.

If there is a slope, you can make the path more interesting by putting in steps. But you should keep in mind what that means for wheelchairs, prams, and other forms of wheeled transport. In such cases, it is better to have a sloping, even path, perhaps with curves. But the main path to the house should always be wide enough for two people to walk abreast.

The most important aspect when designing the area in front of the main entrance is having the proper combination. The paving should suit the house; you must keep in mind the terrain when choosing a route for the path; the choice of plants is determined not only by your taste, but also by their location and function, the season, and the shape and size of the available area. The front gate and front door should harmonise, especially when they are in a direct line with one another and can be seen at the same time when approaching the house.

One factor that is not often taken into consideration is that interesting effects can be achieved with the heights of the plants growing alongside the path to the house. For example, if the front door is higher than the garden and is reached by climbing a few steps, a series of accompanying plants that gradually increase in height can lead up to it most attractively. The house itself can then have climbing plants like clematis growing up the walls and framing the entrance.

Or look at the photograph opposite: the entrance, which is actually rather plain, is given a romantic touch and sense of depth by an arch covered with climbing roses. This pleasant impression of depth is greatly reinforced by the troughs filled with colourful flowers on the small walls to each side of the door, and by the canopy over the door. Hanging flowerpots in the corners also enliven the scene.

However, you can also emphasise a plain entrance by keeping it uncluttered, as in the smaller picture. Some nice greenery on the wall to the right and a few green shrubs on the left are enough to draw one in and lend some structure.

THE FRONT GARDEN PATIO

Neither house nor garden: the patio should be cosy and natural, comfortable and colourful, sheltered and airy – a balancing act that is not really all that difficult. Outdoor living with plants means making room for greenery at the edges and in tubs, as well as some form of paving to provide a firm surface for seating.

Sometimes the patio has to be situated in the front garden: For example, if the house faces south or has a certain shape. The size of the patio, then, of course depends on the space available and how much of it you wish to use for this transitional space between the house and the garden. A patio should be 4 by 2 metres (13 x 7 ft) at minimum, however, to allow room for a table and four chairs and a barbecue corner, as well as for enough greenery.

How about a division of tasks? You can put flowers and flowering plants on and around the patio in front of the house and useful

This front garden, which effortlessly doubles as a patio, is like an outdoor lounge room. Its attractive, cosy appeal will make any visitor want to stay on.

A patio should always have enough room for a table and adequate seating so that you can entertain guests outside in summer. Hanging baskets are particularly attractive.

plants in the real garden at the back. The opposite version is also possible to a degree, but vegetable beds or even berry shrubs directly in front of the lounge room will barely have any space, nor give much visual pleasure. What's more, in winter they are "dead": the beds are empty and the shrubs bare, more like undergrowth.

So let us stick to patios with flowers and green plants. The first question is that of what kind of paving to use. There is an enormous selection, which makes a mixture possible. Different materials create surprisingly charming effects. For example, combining cement pavers and natural stone can be most attractive; cobblestones also fit in well. If you are putting in a new patio, you should leave spaces for grasses, creepers or ground cover plants, which will make stone surfaces look less severe. Here are a few plants you can use in these gaps:

- The flowering hebes are attractive plants; many remain small and have dense, bright green foliage
- 'Prince Charming' carnations are ever-green and flower in summer
- Bugleweed or ajuga, with its purplish leaf rosettes, looks splendid creeping over light-coloured stone
- The soft "cushions" of many plants from the saxifrage family are good for making the edges of the patio seem less severe
- Golden marjoram adds fragrance
- Dead nettles remain small and need little care

But it is larger perennials and shrubs that play the main role on and near the patio. They serve not only to decorate, but also provide protection from inquisitive glances and draughts, particularly in a front garden. You can plant hedges for this purpose, but these are not always suitable for small gardens; it is better to choose mixtures that provide more variety for the eye: here a rare garrya, an evergreen that grows fast and bears grey-green catkins in winter, there a buddleia (also called butterfly bush) with its flower spikes in late summer and autumn. Moveable plants in pots and tubs are also important – from the robust box tree, which can be attractively pruned, to sprawling garlands of flowers from pots hanging on the house wall or a plant-covered frame.

FLOWERS AND PLANTERS

Whether you have room for a garden or your dwelling borders directly on the pavement, you certainly do not have to do without a colourful, flowery welcome. Hanging pots and trailing flowers can always be hung on the facade and under a canopy or overhang. The front light will make sure the plants can be enjoyed even at night.

Hanging flowers suspended in small barrels are particularly decorative around the house entrance. If they are not hung very high, it is better to keep the flowers fairly simple so that the viewer can concentrate on the details of the arrangement.

Windows can be made to seem wider with colourful troughs of flowers, while pots or baskets hanging on brackets or under overhangs give depth to the arrangements. They will brighten up any facade. Depending on how much effort you can or want to spend on hanging gardens, various plants are possible. Petunias, for example, bloom for a particularly long time if they are protected from the rain by a roof, as seen here.

Hanging containers with colourful flowers can serve a number of functions: they can brighten up monotonous facades, make front entrances more inviting, give the trees in your front garden surprising splashes of colour, and lend the front of your house some contour. The higher the baskets or troughs hang, the more flowers they should contain, as their distance from the eye otherwise takes away some of the effect. For this reason, troughs are good to have higher up, as they add a horizontal element that is widely visible. You can hang smaller pots at eye level, because it is the details that are important here. Baskets have one important advantage over pots or troughs: they allow plants to send shoots out through the holes to the sides, something you can prepare for when you put the plants in. However, they need more protection from drying out. This can be done by making a hollowed-out bed of moss and filling it with potting soil mixed with compost. You should also add a granulate that releases water gradually. A small plastic container underneath as a reservoir can also be useful.

The amount of water needed by troughs, baskets and pots depends on their location. If they are exposed to rain, you should check on dry days to see if they are still moist enough. In very bad weather, delicate flowers sometimes have to be taken down temporarily and brought to safety so the roots do not rot because of the stored moisture. Hanging flowerpots under roofs or overhangs should be watered twice a day when it is hot.

Do not be afraid to mix herbs with flowers. They often bloom just as prettily and provide fragrance. They fit well with almost all plants in hanging baskets or pots. Here are some suggestions for plants to use: climbing tuberous begonias, lobelias, colourful verbena varieties, marigolds, climbing fuchsias, large-

flowered petunias, yellow loosestrife with its colourful leaves and yellow flowers, and climbing geraniums.

The flowers are not always what give a combination its charm; some plants have deep green leaves with lighter edges that also add a pleasant touch.

The higher flowers hang, the more luxuriant they can be.

The profusion of blooms on this facade make it stand out even from afar.

SEATING FOR THE GARDEN

You need to be completely at leisure to fully enjoy nature, and that is best achieved when sitting down. The mere sight of somewhere to sit and rest contributes to a sense of well-being. For this reason, benches in the front garden are not just an invitation to stay a while, but also have a decorative function: they stand for comfort and contentment.

When choosing a garden bench, make sure that it fits in harmoniously with its surroundings. Massive, heavy furniture tends to overwhelm a small front garden, while elegant benches are swallowed up by large expanses.

When planning seating areas and where to place benches, you should not only keep practical aspects in mind, but also consider visual effects, both passive and active. You must consider the view you will enjoy from the benches, as well as your ability to see people who approach them. These factors are just as important when placing garden furniture as the aesthetic impression a garden seat will make on those who see it in its setting. First and foremost, however, you should only put in such seating if there is enough room available. In very small front gardens, a bench can be too overpowering and seems rather unimaginative.

There is a large range of garden furniture available in retail stores. When you are trying to make the right choice, your garden and the house before which the bench is to be positioned can give you valuable pointers. Robust, heavy, wooden furniture or stone benches suit a rustic environment. They lose some of their dominance if you plant greenery close to them or place them in a natural niche. More elegant, white, wrought iron seats look very pretty under trees. Single chairs, even quite broad wooden ones, need less room.

If you are good with your hands, you can of course build custom seating yourself. It does not have to be at all complicated. For example, you can place a railway sleeper on top of brick or stone supports, or pile up stones to make a bench. Constructing a circular bench around a tree is more difficult, and would only come into question in a large front garden.

You can simply place a bench in front of the house or at the edge of a path, without much preparation. Admittedly, it looks nicer when it has its own little paved area. This can be a solid surface where a table can be put as well. But it is also most attractive if the paving has gaps with plants growing in them so your feet rest on a soft and natural surface that is still firm underfoot.

A nice view is not the only thing required to create a sense of well-being. Drafts or unpleasant smells will diminish your enjoyment, which is why it is not a good idea to place a bench where there is no shelter from the wind, or too near to the garbage bin. Hedges, small conifers and pergolas can all act as windbreaks. To make sure your time outdoors is an aromatic experience, you can plant herbs directly next to your

favourite place in the front garden: golden sage; sweet, spicy marjoram; various sorts of lemon balm, varieties of mint, or yellow-flowering fennel.

Opposite page: Here, a specially paved area has been built for the bench, separating it optically from the path. This green niche gives the whole arrangement a cosier appearance.

In summer, plantain lilies and hydrangeas in the shade are a feast for the eyes (above).

A street bistro at home (left): furniture like this is ideal for creating a little corner in the front garden for your afternoon coffee. Plants in pots and tubs create a kind of niche.

PATHS IN THE FRONT GARDEN

We have already dealt in detail with the path leading to the front door. But larger front gardens also need side paths to provide access to more remote flowerbeds, to go around ponds, or to reach the hedges, which need to be pruned every now and then. This small network of paths deserves your attention as a structural element in your garden.

Paths simultaneously divide and connect different areas of a garden. From a utilitarian perspective, they are used to reach outbuildings (tool shed, garage, garden house, and so on), they separate plant borders from the lawn, cut through the latter, and may even lead by way of a few steps to a rock garden on a higher level. All of this will only be possible in small doses in your front gar-

den, but because this is the part of your outdoor space most on view, even short paths should be given due respect.

A simple paved path can easily be made more attractive by luxuriant growth beside it, but it is better as a "main road" than as a small "side street". Bricks, which are also a little severe but add attractive colour and are more versatile due to their fine patterning, suit rustic front

> Garden paths primarily have a connecting function, but there is no reason for them to be unaesthetic. They can—and should—be made to blend harmoniously into their surroundings. The choice of the right surface is very important. A good way to set off a path in a dense garden is to put in arched trellises, which act as markers, particularly when the plants covering them are in bloom.

gardens as well as more formal ones. If you have the option, it is lovely to use old bricks that are perhaps a little weathered; they have more "tales to tell" than new, shiny ones. The latter can be used to good purpose near ponds, for example, because they will not absorb moisture.

There is no need to describe the advantages of natural stone again here. Let it just be said that it is particularly recommended for side paths and—like gravel, stepping stones and timber paths—natural stone gives the front garden a natural appearance. Strangely enough, mowed lawn paths look more artificial and should only be considered if your aim is to intensify the impression of green or you want to give a sense of softness. They fit in well between small fruit trees and in meadow-like areas.

As these comments on lawn paths clearly show, the choice of materials and the positioning of paths is always dependent in part on the surroundings. Side paths should be fairly unobtrusive and convey an intimate impression. If they are overgrown here and there by plants, and wind their way through shrubs, this objective is achieved. Grass growing between paving stones or wooden sleepers is not at all undesirable, indeed, it increases a path's charm.

Ground covers at the edges of paths have the tendency to spill out onto the paths themselves, which makes them a good choice. If they are properly selected, they also provide a colourful border: lady's mantle, with its delicate leaves, makes for a soft edge; the shoots of ground ivy will grow up steps; mats of purple rock cress and the pink blossoms of bergenias are harbingers of spring; and wintergreen will bear red berries and leaves well into winter.

Ground covers not only provide borders for paths, they also blur the distinction between it and the rest of the garden, making for a smooth, natural transition (left).

The irregularities in paths made of natural stone (below) can make a front garden seem more natural. You can also put in low steps.

THE USES OF IVY

Many people find ivy too conservative, while it puts others in mind of cemeteries. Both of these attitudes are prejudices born of an ignorance about the wide range of ivy available. You can obtain this plant with all kinds of different leaves and in a broad variety of colours. This offers possibilities that are often left unused.

Even different kinds of ivy growing next to each other create a lively impression. But ivy is also very sociable, and gets along well with other climbing plants such as clematis and nasturtiums. Their blossoms combine with the jagged, beautifully patterned leaves of ivy to make a perfect ensemble. A wall of solid ivy can also be broken up and enlivened by slender conifers like juniper or arborvitae.

Here are some of the things that ivy can do: it attaches itself to walls on its own and doesn't need any supports. Many varieties grow well in the shade, so they are a good option for decorating northern walls, where only a few other plants are as happy. What is more, it also provides a certain amount of insulation, something that is often forgotten.

Because it loves to climb, it soon hides unsightly walls and fences or other constructions like garbage-bin enclosures, carports, garages and sheds. It can provide excellent screens for privacy or wind protection when grown on frames. As ground cover, ivy keeps weeds under bushes at bay and creates "carpets". It softens any edges, takes gardens into the third dimension, turns old tree stumps or posts into fantastic figures and, when properly trained, is a top-class "sculptor".

In addition, you can have as much ivy as you want, when you want it. All you have to do is make sure that it propagates enough, and that

> Ivy willingly hides and decorates garages, sheds, and walls without needing much assistance: it doesn't require any supports and propagates easily.

is not difficult. In late summer, cut offsets from the soft tips of the shoots, dip the cut edges into some rooting powder and place them in a pot with compost that contains gravel. Another method is to cover an ivy shoot with soil. It will put out roots, a process you can encourage by taking off the bark on the underside. When you remove the soil the next spring, you can just separate the new plant from its parent and plant it where you need new ivy.

Here is a just small selection of the range of ivy varieties that can be obtained in specialist garden centres: 'Filigree' is a type of ivy that has medium-green, round, crinkly leaves; 'Glacier' has grey-green leaves with creamy margins; 'Bill Archer', a bushy variety, has unusually long and narrow leaves; 'Goldchild' is well-named for its leaves with their glowing yellow edges; 'Hummingbird', as the name would suggest, loves sun and has green and white speckled leaves; 'Gloire de Marengo' has large leaves with silver edges and will climb even the highest walls with ease.

Ivy does not have to be used on its own. It harmonises well with flowering plants (above).

Who knew a garbage bin could look so pretty (left)? Placing it in an ivy-covered enclosure is a discreet and aesthetic solution that will greatly improve the appearance of your front garden.

ROCK
GARDENS

WALLS GREAT AND SMALL

Even a small garden needs borders and elements to give it structure. Walls, both large and small, are a good choice here. They give verticality to otherwise horizontal surroundings and look extremely attractive when covered with plants and flowers. The stone and plants can either be contrasting or chosen to complement each either.

> Drystone walls do not necessarily have to make a "dry" impression. Adorned with sweet alyssum and evergreen candytuft, for example, any wall is transformed into a feast for the eye.

There are various possibilities for decorating garden walls, depending on the height of the wall. A high surrounding wall covered in an evergreen coat of ivy or other climbers is a very restful sight. If you want something more lively, you can break it up a little using dog roses, jasmine or plants for wall niches. High walls in the sun are ideal for mountain plants, while those in the shade look very natural with ferns. In the case of such high walls, or the walls of a house, you can choose between plants that attach themselves to walls and climb without any help or creepers that need wires, nets or a trellis. It is advisable to use the latter if the wall needs to be painted every so often. Then you can move the trellis away and attach it again when you are finished without too much effort. A particularly attractive effect is achieved when vegetation covers arched gateways or sections of fencing. Here are some good plants for high walls:

- Vines that have flame-coloured foliage in autumn
- Firethorn, which bears blossoms in summer and berries in winter
- Common knotgrass, one of the fastest-growing and most successful covering plants

- Climbing hydrangeas, which are good for shady northern sides
- Blue blossom, a colourful plant for sheltered locations.

Smaller walls are most often used to divide a garden into distinct areas, or as borders for raised beds, sometimes even on several levels. If the wall is freestanding and well prepared with suitable soil in its cracks and joints, colourful alpine plants will grow well on them. Particularly in small gardens, walls create welcome additional space for vegetation. Hanging plants provide elegant decoration for wall copings. Drystone walls are also ideal biotopes for small animals like lizards, which take advantage of the warmth stored in the stone. The flowers will attract bees and butterflies.

The following plants are good for wall niches:
- Various types of stonecrop, as they form dense mats
- Siskiyou lewsia, which forms tufts and has delicate pink blossoms in early summer
- Erigerons, with their daisy-like heads
- Houseleek, which forms carpets
- Maidenhair spleenwort, which can even tolerate direct sunlight
- Saxifrage, which in spring produces bright yellow "cushions".

When you first construct the walls, it is very important to make sure they are stable by building them with the heavier stones at the bottom and the lighter ones at the top. If walls are over a half a metre (20 in) tall, a firm foundation will make them safer. The main danger is the force of water, so you should make sure it is able to drain away. Lay out a gravel bed or even a proper drainage system at the base of the wall, particularly if it is situated at the bottom of a slope.

Rock cress (above), with its intense violet-coloured flowers, is one plant that makes old walls or stones particularly striking.

The luxuriant mats formed by most rock-garden plants will quickly cover even difficult surfaces such as niches and joints in walls.

A TERRACED GARDEN

Terracing enlivens even the smallest garden. The different levels make it possible to create variety through contrasts of colour and form. If your plot is on a slope, it is only a question of giving it an attractive layout. Otherwise, you can build a small "mountain range" to your own design and use stones to give support to the various levels.

There are many models to emulate in the world around us—for rock gardens, too. For example, for centuries drystone walling has been used in vineyards to support walls. This gives rise to terraces, particularly on steep slopes. You can imitate these structures in your rock garden.

Whether a slope is natural or human-made, it provides abundant gardening opportunities. You can even put in lawns, though they are more difficult to grow here than on a flat area. Prepare the ground as usual and compact it using a roller or—if the slope is too steep—with the back of a rake. Then put down rolls of turf (available in some garden centres, but easily ordered from a reliable supplier who will deliver them to you) on the chosen piece of garden. Use sections that are not too large, as they might slip. If needed, pin the strips down until they have taken root.

Evergreen elegance is provided by conifers and varieties of heather, which spread quickly and give colour to green areas. When putting them in, you can hinder weeds by placing a sheet of plastic on the prepared ground. Cut cross-shaped slits in the plastic in the right spots and plant the seedlings through these. The plastic also gives support to steep slopes until the plants are firmly established.

Naturally, you will require paths or places to stand among your hilly landscape so you can carry out routine activities such as watering and weeding. You could put in the usual steps, but another interesting and natural looking option is to use tree trunks in various ways. They can be put down lengthwise as steps, and the space to the next step filled with earth, paving, gravel, or slate scree. Thicker trunks can be cut into rounds of the desired height and put down singly or in rows stepwise up the slope. Thin posts driven vertically into the ground very close to one another can be used to form a sort of banister, which can be also covered in greenery.

A terraced garden with paths and steps provides several different levels for growing things. These levels can be subdivided still further by means of stones of different shapes and sizes. The choice of plants can also make a contribution, as dwarf conifers, bushes and small trees give vertical structure, while creepers lend softer contours to the whole.

Some of the plants that are good choices for shady slopes are:

- Scurvygrass, a ground covering plant with abundant flowers
- Singleseed juniper, a dense shrub
- Stinking hellebore, which has an ugly name, but blooms even in the deepest wintertime
- Yellow-flowered barberry, whose low varieties are well suited to slopes and rock gardens
- Skimmias, whose buds glow red in winter and whose blossoms peep out from the green foliage like snowballs in spring.

Steep slopes need to be well secured so that stones do not slide down. If the slope is less dramatic (as above) you may wish to build a terrace on the same level. But even here you must make sure there is good support so that the slope does not start sliding.

PLANTING A ROCK GARDEN

The saying "opposites attract" can also be applied to gardens. Massive stones and barren scree provide an effective background for floral beauty. Slender grasses and compact bushy plants also produce lovely contrasts of both shape and colour, as do colourful clumps of flowers and jagged rocks.

Huge boulders can be rather overwhelming, but you don't have to use big chunks of stone. In a mini-rock garden, it is often a better idea to stick with the proportions of your garden and use smaller specimens.

You have achieved the right effect when you create by design that which nature produces on its own in the mountains. For this reason, the plants you choose should be put in so they look self-sown. Even carefully arranged compositions of colour and form should look natural. Typical rock-garden plants, often very small but with luxuriant foliage and delicate flowers, create a particularly good effect in these surroundings. Plan carefully where the various plants are to be placed. For instance, creeping plants should have enough room to spread over rocks and slopes. Straight shrubs and bushes will give your rock garden height. Rocks, scree and gravel play a subordinate role to the vegetation, which will look all the more vital and elegant when displayed against an austere background.

A scree bed is a good place for imitating the kind of terrain found in mountainous regions. Rubble made up of variously sized rock fragments lies on

Old stone grinding troughs with pretty plants in them are an eye-catcher in any rock garden. They need to have drainage holes so that water does not collect in them.

Tuff is very porous and thus not as heavy as other types of stone. Because it stores water, plants grow well right around it.

moist soil and forms gaps where plants can grow. This is where you can help a little. Mostly, dainty plants like those of the saxifrage family are the ones that grow well here. Here are a few tips for creating a scree bed:

- Mark off the area first with string and stakes. Dig out a hollow bed around 40 cm (15 in) deep. Fill the hole halfway with undressed stone or building rubble, spreading it evenly. Cover this layer with turf that you have either previously cut from the site or bought, with the grass facing downward.

- Put in a scree mixture consisting of one part soil and one part peat (peat substitute is even better) to three parts coarse sand or grit. Tread it down well and water it so that it is moist all the way through. Put in the plants you desire and then put on a covering layer of scree, pushing some right under the leaves of the young plants to make it seem as though they are growing straight out of the rock.

One of the main charms of a rock garden is exactly that: observing how plants manage to thrive in apparently hostile surrroundings.

Flowering plants growing out of crevices and niches among the rocks and stones are a particularly refreshing sight.

Here are some tips for vertical crevices:

- Scrape out any detritus with a knife or a trowel. Wedge in a small stone at the bottom of the crevice as a support for the soil. Put a substrate consisting of soil, leaf mould, garden compost and coarse gravel (to provide water drainage) into the crevice. After putting in the plant, press down the soil around its roots with your fingertips.

ALPINE PLANTS

Even if there is little room and it is not possible to put in a sloping rock garden, you will always find a little corner somewhere in the yard for the small alpine plants—even in the middle of a paved patio. You can use or make gaps between the pavers for growing colourful clumps of flowers or even taller herbaceous perennials.

Seats, quiet areas or patios can all be integrated into a rock garden. Not only the plants are important in this respect, but also the combination of materials used and the planning of the whole so that it doesn't look artificial.

An unbroken surface of cement or asphalt is anathema to any keen gardener. Fortunately, most owners of yards and patios no longer put one down, even though this sometimes necessitates putting in drainage so that the subsoil does not get too moist. And if an area does have to be completely sealed, your alpine flowers can be displayed to decorative effect in troughs or raised beds.

However, it is more attractive when mountain plants grow directly out of the stone, as they do on rock faces or amid gravel in the wild. If paving has already been put in, you are sure to be able to find a crack somewhere that you can widen or remove stones from. You can then scrape out the crevice to make it deeper and fill it with special rock-garden soil, available at your garden centre. Seeds or small flowers can be planted in it. Grass thrives particularly

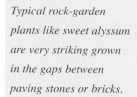

Stonecrop is particularly good for bordering a patio.

well in such crevices. But be careful what you choose. Some types have such strong roots that they can break up the stone around the crack. The expansion and contraction of the soil due to freezing and thawing during the winter months can compound the problem.

But this may not trouble you at all. If it does happen, you will eventually have larger gaps in the paving. Then you can plant a merry company of alpine plants, making your yard into a rock garden or mountain plateau landscape. If you keep the plant growth under control, these undemanding plants will not try to encroach on your seating area. Because patios are mostly on raised ground, they are particularly suitable for small alpine plants, as water will drain well if the ground underneath is at all permeable. Normally pavers are placed on a bed of gravel, so lack of drainage is unlikely to be a problem. It is of course easiest to create plant-covered yards, patios, or paved paths like this if you can prepare the right conditions when they are being built. You can decide at the start where the gaps for plants are to be and prepare the soil there appropriately. There may then even be room for dwarf shrubs and spreading ground cover. Climbers can grow up special

supports and varieties of heather will provide long-lasting colour.

Here are some of the larger alpine plants that are good for such purposes:

- Dwarf broom, with its pea-shaped flowers and tiny leaves
- Dwarf forsythias, which can grow to 40 cm (15 in) in height
- Ivy, with its pointed leaves
- Evergreen holly
- Types of box that grow to be only some 20 cm (8 in) high.

Of course, these larger plants will only look really good if the garden is fairly sizeable.

Typical rock-garden plants like sweet alyssum are very striking grown in the gaps between paving stones or bricks.

Japanese rock gardens and dry gardens have a long tradition. They differ greatly from western gardens both aesthetically and structurally. They are ideal for small spaces. Here the fundamental principle is that less is more.

LAYING OUT A ROCK GARDEN

Many plants that would go unnoticed in busy flower beds have a striking effect in a carefully designed rock garden. Mixtures of small flowering plants or even grass varieties contrast strongly with the browns, greys and ochres of their surroundings and both are shown to advantage, the durable stone and its colourful living counterparts.

Stones have been with us since the beginning of time, and the first thing you should consider when planning a rock garden is where to place them. They provide the framework for the plants that will grow between them, on them and around them. Of course, this framework is mobile, as the stones, particularly the smaller ones, can always be moved to different positions. But the basic layout will remain fairly constant, especially if you are also considering having shrubs or permanent herbaceous plants.

When constructing a rock garden, gardeners usually try to keep as close as possible to natural models. However, this is not the only option. Natural does not necessarily mean arbitrary, so careful arrangement and artistic creativity can also play a part. You can con-

deep and should be spread under the leaves of the plants. This protects against rot. Renew the layer every so often by removing the gravel and soil from around the plants and putting in a fresh mixture. If there are any weeds, remove the intruders together with their roots and put new gravel on the affected area.

Coarse gravel, perhaps with some areas of lawn or paving stones, can bring some colour to the arrangement, as the stones that make it up are all of different hues. At the same time, they are small enough to give a uniform background, ideal as a canvas for your chosen stones and plants.

Green and grey, bright colours and brown should form a coherent whole. Keeping everything compact helps achieve this aim. The plants can be arranged together as islands, but should sometimes also emerge directly from the stone. There are types of limestone that are extremely porous and retain water; if the stones have hollows that can be filled with soil, plants can grow directly on them.

Exuberant splendour or the stark serenity of a few essentials— minimalist rock gardens are certainly not to everybody's taste, but they do exude a certain fascination all the same.

sider the soil a canvas upon which you will create your artwork. This can also be understood in a spatial sense, for as a modern artist, you will not confine yourself to two dimensions; your material, stones and plants, will in themselves introduce an element of depth to the work. Your canvas may be allowed to fall in folds and be spread over uneven terrain.

This brings us to the "undercoat", that is, the top layer upon which the stones will lie, in which they will be embedded, over which they will be strewn or upon which they can be arranged geometrically. Gravel makes for a good top layer; it also provides good drainage. This is important, as typical rock garden plants do not like things too moist as a rule.

Here are a few tips regarding the top layer: the gravel should only applied 1 to 3 cm (½–1 in)

PATHS THROUGH ROCK GARDENS

Basically, the same principles apply to building paths in rock gardens as in any other garden setting. An additional consideration, however, is how to get from one level to the other and what kind of path best fits the surroundings. You cannot go wrong using natural stone. It will only enhance the desired effect.

Straight lines are not characteristic of a natural rock garden. When laying out paths in one, avoid making them overly uniform and even. Try to choose natural materials that suit the surroundings.

Paths and steps, and perhaps single paving stones here and there, should give access to all areas of the garden, of course, but they also have important structural and visual functions. This means both aesthetic and practical considerations must be taken into account when planning the paths through your rocky Eden. The most important principle here is that the harmonious arrangement of stones and plants is primary and should be designed first, and only then should you plan the pathways through or around it.

For areas that don't have to be accessible with a wheelbarrow or other unwieldy equipment, it generally suffices to have stepping stones or narrow gravel paths. These are unobtrusive and fit well with the stone landscape. If a rock garden is only one part of your small garden, it can easily be separated from other areas by a broader path. You can also emphasise the transition from one section to another by using different paving materials.

The steeper the slope your garden is on, the more frequently you will have to put in steps. They give vertical contour. If they are curved or even in a zigzag, they will enhance the impression of a mountain landscape, as will winding paths without steps. The latter should be preferred if wheelbarrows, prams or anything else that is difficult to get up steps are used in the garden. Aesthetically speaking, massive stone steps emphasise ruggedness, while curving paths serve to soften contours.

You can also achieve this softer look by making steps of natural stone deliberately uneven and edging them with plants. Ground cover and creepers are the most suitable plants for this purpose; their greenness and colour will render the hard stone more pleasing to the eye and soften transitions. They look particularly good in rock gardens sprouting forth from gaps in steps or between paving stones. Be sure to leave room for them while building the steps.

All of the many small plants that grow elsewhere in rock gardens are suitable for such locations. You can have carpets of saxifrage rosettes at the edge of the steps, greyish green snow-in-summer in sunny spots, purple rock cress or sweet alyssum. Banisters can also add interest, not only on steep steps, but also crossing small gaps or ponds. When covered with creepers, they are extremely decorative.

If there is enough room in your small garden, a path can also widen to form a circular or oval space. A bench placed here will be an invitation to you and others to rest and enjoy the sight of your stone paradise.

Slopes present special challenges when designing paths. But you don't always have to resort to steps; large stone pavers can also be used.

TREES AND SHRUBS IN ROCK GARDENS

Trees in a small rock garden? Don't worry: the idea is not to turn your rock garden into a mountain forest. The following brief portraits introduce some of the larger and taller plants you can use as highlights. Of course, you must limit yourself to dwarf versions of trees and shrubs. Interestingly, in some settings they can have the impact of full-sized trees in comparison with the tiny alpine flowers that are their neighbours.

The ground covering plants and creepers, bushy flowers and green carpets of ground covering plants in your rock garden will disappear in winter as soon as snow falls. This can make an elegantly designed landscape look like a pale hill that soon turns an unsightly grey owing to the ubiquitous air pollution.

You can avoid this impression by planting a few trees or shrubs. Conifers will always provide a little green, while the bare branches of deciduous trees, with their sometimes acrobatic gestures, will tell in mime of the coming spring.

Unfortunately, many a rock gardener has had unpleasant surprises with trees or shrubs that did not remain as nice and small as they were when first purchased. Make sure to always find out what height trees are likely to attain! Otherwise you may end up with almost uncontrollable undergrowth that spreads out and takes over valuable space that could be used for flowers.

When deciding where to put small shrubs or trees, you should think about their function and the overall effect: if you need shelter from the wind for a delicate corner of the garden, there are those that will do the job reliably. Of course, they will also create shade, something many rock-garden plants do not like. You will have to weigh up shelter against shade. In many cases, you will probably decide against having the particular shrub or tree.

There is another factor that merits consideration. Trees and shrubs, as we have already said, act as highlights. For this reason, they should receive the most attention when you are planning and planting your rock garden. Because they are most difficult to move once they have taken root, they should be put in first. Of course, this should not be at the "summit" of your small mountain, but in the lower-lying part. Here is a short list of suitable plants:

ALPINE ROSE

You probably know this shrub by the name rhododendron, and envision huge flowering bushes that may be larger than your entire garden.

Of course, it isn't those big evergreens that are meant here, but the dwarf version, which grows wild as the alpine rose (a low shrub) in mountainous regions. This small bush grows up to 40 cm (15 in), or in some cases 80 cm (30 in), and is thus barely higher than many ornamental grasses or perennials.

These plants, like all members of the heath family, do not usually grow well in chalky soil, and too much sun is unfavourable for them as well. But they are rather thirsty, even in winter, when their leathery leaves give off large amounts of moisture. This doesn't mean they need to be drowned, however. It is enough to keep the soil near the roots constantly moist. If you want a plant that blooms late in the year, you should try a hedgehog rose. They only grow to about 25 cm (10 in) high, so keep this in mind if what you require is a medium-sized shrub.

HEATHER

Heather is often not recognised as being one of the woody plants, and as far as its height is concerned, common heather is often more like a ground cover. But if you should try to break off a branch of it, you will see that woody it is, and fairly tough wood at that.

This is what makes heather so popular with rock gardeners, as it is undemanding yet enormously resilient. It will grow without complaint even on barren, sandy soil that has a low chalk content, whether dry or moist. The only thing it doesn't tolerate is too much frost.

There are some heather cultivars that behave more like shrubs. A few can even grow to 1 metre (3 ft) in height. They blossom in late summer and autumn and retain some colour for a long time after this.

Prune back heather plants every year after they have blossomed. In their natural setting, they are likely to be trimmed back by sheep.

SPRUCE

Most people are only familiar with this tree as a 50-metre (160-ft) high denizen of the woods, and even the types most frequently encountered in gardens reach a height of 10 to 20 metres (30 to 65 ft).

Of course, these sorts are out of the question for small gardens, let alone rock gardens. But spruce also exists in shorter, cultivated forms.

One of these, the dwarf 'Pumila' spruce, is probably still too large for a small rockery, growing up to 2 metres (7 ft). But other dwarf spruces, such as the Pygmaea Norway spruce, are much more suitable. The Pygmaea grows 1 metre (3 feet) high and looks like a Christmas tree. If your rock garden graces the front of your house, you could even string your Pygmaea with lights for some holiday cheer. For an even smaller tree, choose the hedgehog spruce. As its name suggests, it forms thick cushions of needles about 60 cm (2 feet) high.

WINTER HEATH

Winter heath or true heath, a European native, is only 30 cm (12 in) high but very impressive for all that. It's a member of the erica family, like heather, but winter heath belongs to genus *Erica* as well. It is one of few in its family that grows on chalky soil, but accepts acidic ground. Heath blooms when little else does: its first bell-like flowers may appear in February. They are normally pink, but some cultivars have white or red flowers. The sunnier a snowy landscape is, the better.

Some cultivars blossom at other times and grow taller than these tiny shrubs. One sort stands ca. 60 cm (24 in) high, has narrow leaves on four-sided branches and bears pink blossoms from March to May. Cornish heath reaches a similar size. In sheltered spots, this plant is hardy and blooms pink from July to September.

Because of winter heath's various bloom times and foliage colours, if you choose carefully you can almost always have some colour in a heath garden. Cross-leaved heath will bloom with particularly pretty flowers if it is planted in sandy loam with some peat. Pruning it after it has blossomed promotes flowering in the next year. This erica can be propagated with 4-cm (1½-in) offshoots. After a month under plastic sheeting, these will put out roots and can be planted.

BROOM

If you put in a clever mix of broom varieties, you can enjoy its small, delicate blossoms from May until early autumn. These undemanding but attractive plants have small dark green leaves that provide colour even when they are not in bloom. *Genista anglica* (literally, "English broom"), known as petty whin, grows to ca. 60 cm (24 in) high and bears its thorns and blossoms in upright clusters. *Genista pilosa*, or hairy green-weed, is smaller and thus better for rock gardens. It only reaches 40 cm (15 in). It is considered a wild flower in the U.K., so make sure you aquire it legitimately. It will be heartier in the garden if nursery grown. Other small types are winged broom, a creeper, and Spanish broom, a small shrub that reaches 60 cm (2 ft). All of these have yellow blossoms.

ST JOHNSWORT

You have many varieties to choose from if you decide to plant St Johnswort shrubs. There are some 200 different sorts, which only stand between 30 cm (12 in) and 1 metre (3 ft) tall.

The plant's name comes from the folk custom of wearing garlands of the flowers for midsummer celebrations on St John's Day. Bonfires were lit and young people danced around them. When the festive fires went out, the dancers threw the garlands on the roofs of their houses; this was thought to be a sure protection against lightning.

For very small gardens, only the St Johnswort shrubs that grow up to 20 cm (8 in) high are to be

recommended. They are quite compact and in summer bear yellow, slightly dotted flowers, often united in bundles. If you have more room, these robust plants are also available as shrubs of up to 1 metre (3 ft) in height. Their reddish stems have egg-shaped, smooth-margined, tough leaves that are greenish-blue underneath. There are overhanging varieties like 'Forrestii' and ones that grow upright like 'Henryi', which has somewhat smaller leaves.

St Johnswort plants need to be sheltered from frost in winter. They should be pruned regularly after blooming, so that the plants will grow strong and sturdy.

PINE

This is a tree that is extremely undemanding and adaptable, but also immensely tall for the proportions at hand in small gardens. The types found in forests from the Mediterranean to North Cape can reach heights of 50 metres (165 ft) and more. Happily for gardeners, more than 80 other sorts have been developed, some of which are perfectly suitable for the small garden.

The mountain pine, for example, which is found in nature at the timberline (around 2,500 metres/8,200 feet above sea level) is only as large as a shrub and is therefore the best candidate for your small rock garden. It grows well on embankments and can also be planted in containers. If you choose to have a potted pine, you must make sure the soil never remains saturated, as the

roots may otherwise rot. A layer of gravel and broken flower pots can help rainwater drain. The dwarf pine only grows to 1 metre (3 ft) in height. With its trailing branches, it also looks very shrub-like. Other recommended dwarf pines are the varieties 'Pumilio' and 'Schmidtii', which have a nice rounded shape. You may well have to spend some time looking for these trees, as only a few nurseries and large garden centres stock them.

ARBORVITAE

The arborvitae (thuja) was introduced to Europe from North America in the sixteenth century. It likes semi-shaded locations and sandy, loamy soil. In its place of origin, there are specimens that are up to 60 metres (200 ft) tall. In Europe it can still grow to 30 metres (100 ft). However, varieties have now been cultivated that are an ideal size for your small garden. For example, the Korean arborvitae is only 1.5 metres (5 ft) tall when fully grown. It has trailing reddish brown branches and is similar to the weeping variety, 'Pendula', whose fresh

green leaves turn brownish in winter. The 'Pumila' variety has a rounded shape, while 'Rosenthali' is conical in form. And there are some sorts that even only develop into ground cover. This evergreen tree grows together to form thick hedges, but is also attractive on its own. It fills the surrounding atmosphere with a pleasantly aromatic fragrance, which can be smelt very intensely if you rub the scale-like leaves between your fingers. These leaves only grow on older trees, however; the young plants have needle-shaped foliage.

DAPHNE

In the case of daphnes, you can choose between evergreen or deciduous kinds. There are approximately 70 varieties available. Daphne shrubs are similar to laurels. They owe their name to the nymph in ancient Greek mythology who, pursued by the love-maddened Apollo, avoided his advances by being transformed into the tree that bears her name. Her escape was thorough indeed, as all parts of the tree, from the bark to its fruit, are poisonous. Ten berries are enough to kill a person.

The best-known deciduous variety is the alpine daphne, which grows to a height of between 1 and 1.5 metres (3–5 ft). Its leaves are hairy on both sides. In May or June it produces white blossoms with an intensive fragrance.

Rose daphne, on the other hand, is an evergreen. It only grows 30 cm (12 in) high, has spatula-shaped leaves, and produces red, fragrant clusters of blossoms, also in May/June. It grows well in stony, dry and chalky soil.

YEW

In ancient times, the original European forests consisted to a large extent of yews, which have the botanical name *Taxus*. They were considered sacred, and priests often used to carry out their sacred rituals in yew groves. The needles of these evergreen conifers are so thick that almost sunlight can penetrate them only with difficulty. Where several yews are standing close together, they produce a twilight that encourages reflection.

Yews are trees that grow very slowly and reach an enormous age. Individual specimens as much as 2,000 years old have been found. In addition to their thick, soft needles, they bear bright red fruits. These look like berries, but are in fact arils, or seed coverings. Interestingly, they are the only part of the tree that is not poisonous. These "berries" are very popular with birds, which help spread the seeds and thus, propagate the plant anew.

Small, slender varieties of yew have been cultivated. These will fit well into your rock garden and give it some contour. Being very undemanding, yews are well suited to rockeries. There are also varieties with creeping or trailing branches. They tolerate both shade and direct sunlight and are grateful simply to be provided with slightly moist, chalky soil.

JUNIPER

This tree, a member of the cypress family, may well owe its popularity to the fact that it brings some "Mediterranean" flair to our cooler and moister climate. Many rock gardeners also choose junipers to give a heath-like corner a more natural look.

After all, this evergreen conifer originates from heath regions. As a result, it is not very demanding with regard to soil conditions, and can tolerate either sun or shade.

The medicinal properties of its sweet berries have made juniper much prized, and the fact that they can be turned into gin and geneva has also certainly done this plant's reputation no harm. There are several dwarf varieties suited to your rock garden. Creeping juniper, which fully lives up to its name, deserves a special mention. It grows to a height of only some 30 cm (12 in). When young, its long branches bear bluish green needles, and later scale-like leaves. They creep over the ground and form shoot-like roots. In this way, the plants can cover quite large areas.

COTONEASTER

This is another member of the large and noble rose family that can join the decorative shrubs in your rock garden. Cotoneasters are available in very small varieties. They are particularly suitable for planting borders, creating a colourful framework consisting of garlands of white or pink flowers in summer. In autumn, they produce dense clusters of bright red berries.

In a very shady location the cotoneaster cannot be seen to advantage, and most forms of the plant do not grow well in them, either. It grows well in sun or partial shade. Cotoneaster definitely appreciates soil that is well drained, as too much moisture is fatal to it. You can use a creeping variety such as *Cotoneaster dammeri* (up to 20 cm/8 in tall) to form evergreen carpets.

HERBACEOUS PERENNIALS IN ROCK GARDENS

Herbaceous perennials are the group of plants with the widest variety of types, shapes, and colours. An almost countless number of them are suitable for small rock gardens. They often need little soil, but grow for years, producing abundant flowers or cushions of greenery. Combined with shrubs and trees, they can create very attractive effects.

The herbaceous perennials are a large group of plants whose top growth dies down to the ground in autumn, while the roots survive the winter to grow anew in spring. Some perennials even remain green in the winter.

Anybody who studies these wonders of nature more closely will see that perennial plants form an almost inexhaustible area of study with regard to their characteristics, differing needs for light and soil types, their nutritional and watering requirements, methods of planting, and so on. Their variety is almost endless.

Here we shall only be looking at the question of what perennials are suitable for rock gardens. We provide a short list of the plants that are most commonly used for this purpose, along with short portraits of each and a few tips for rock gardeners.

A good general rule is: plants that flower in spring should be planted in autumn and vice versa. Plants that have grown too big can normally be divided and replanted; gardeners know, of course, that you should avoid damaging the roots. With some perennials you should be sparing with the fertiliser. With most of them it is enough to work some thoroughly decomposed compost into the soil between the plants twice a year.

You should tie large plants to a support before they get too big, as they are often too heavy to withstand strong gusts of wind or rainstorms. Pests are not much of a problem if you make sure the soil is right and the plants receive nutrition (in the form of compost and other fertilisers) in proper doses. You can use sand to keep snails and slugs away from delphiniums or lupines.

These basic questions of care and maintenance are not as difficult to answer as those regarding which perennials to use in which combinations and the effect they can produce when mixed with shrubs. You can ask experienced rock gardeners for advice, but will soon find that you can only create your dream garden when you've gathered some experience and discovered your own, very personal taste, the most important factor.

AQUILEGIA

The aquilegia or columbine is one of the most tolerant perennials. Its name comes from Latin and means "water collector," a reference to the plant's succulent stem. It grows well in both partial shade and sunny locations. Together with anemones, chrysanthemums and other summer flowers it forms not only magnificent herbaceous borders, but also wonderful bouquets. In a rock garden, aquilegias prefer to be planted in rocky niches or near dwarf trees and shrubs.

The already very numerous wild varieties of aquilegia have been cultivated to produce an immeasurably vast number of garden varieties. There are some to suit every garden: plants that grow only a few centimetres tall, and others that stretch up to a metre (3 ft) high.

All of the wild aquilegias bear flowers with a characteristic spur, while cultivation has produced some types that do not have one. Cultivated varieties also come in a wide range of colours: you have the choice of white, blue, red, yellow, purple and even multi-coloured flowers that catch the eye wherever they are situated.

ASTER

The aster is one of the most popular perennials for the garden and should not be absent from a rock garden either. The question is only one of choice, for there is a huge range of varieties, shapes and colours to select from—a plant for every season. Among the tallest of the spring-blooming asters are the varieties 'Wartburgstern' and 'Berggarten.' The name of the latter ("mountain garden") indicates its suitability for rock gardens and suggests the beauty of the flowers. It grows up to 50 cm (20 in) tall and is surmounted by large purple flowers with a yellow centre. Rock gardeners may want something a bit smaller. In this case, they can use a variety that is crossed with the alpine aster. It raises its purple head just 10 cm (4 in) high and is good for borders.

Italian aster and heath aster blossom in late summer and autumn. The former has lavender flowers, the latter, white radial ones. The white, pink and purple flowers of dwarf aromatic asters will last until the first frost comes.

EDELWEISS

You cannot really imitate a mountainous terrain without the most typical alpine plant of all: edelweiss, the very symbol of the mountains. The popularity of this plant actually endangered it, as mountain travellers all wanted to stick one on their hat or in their buttonhole. Alpine edelweiss is, however, rather disappointing in a garden. But rock gardeners can still enjoy this whitish yellow gem of a flower, as there are many cultivated forms of Asiatic species available. They only grow 1.5 cm (½ in) tall. A typical characteristic is a thick, white fuzz on their leaves and flowers. This protects the plant, which prefers to be in direct sunlight, from receiving too much of the sun's rays and also prevents excessive evaporation.

As with all plants of the composite family, its flowers occur in heads, several of which are joined together to form dense, flower-like clusters. What appears to be their "petals" have a lance-like shape and are, in fact, extremely woolly, white leaves. Edelweiss likes permeable, chalky, gravelly soil.

GENTIAN

Perhaps the most popular alpine plant after edelweiss is gentian. The intense blue colouring of its bell-like flowers makes a really strong impression only when several plants are seen near one another. For this reason, gentian should be planted in groups in locations that receive a good deal of sun. Many garden varieties of gentian have been cultivated, so there are suitable ones for every rock garden. For example, there is trumpet gentian, which forms thick green cushions and flowers from May onwards. The unique flowers, which can be up to 5 cm (2 in) deep, have an incomparable, velvety blue colouring.

Willow gentian, on the other hand, is a giant in comparison, reaching heights of up to 90 cm (3 ft). Its flowers are not much larger than its smaller cousins', but have purple spots inside. Almost all varieties of gentian require sunny or semi-shaded locations.

CINQUEFOIL

You can enjoy the abundant flowers of the different cinquefoil varieties from March to September. This member of the noble rose family is available in many different species and forms that particularly suit rock gardens.

Its name comes from a French word meaning "five-leaf"; many varieties have toothed leaves divided into five to seven leaflets. It used to be particularly prized as a remedy for bowel, liver and kidney complaints. Though no longer used as medicine, cinquefoil is now a popular ornamental for rock gardens, where some varieties are excellent, low-maintenance ground cover. It grows anywhere from a few centimetres to 1.5 metres (1 in–5 ft). Any of the many kinds that boast large, bright red flowers will add striking colour to your garden.

LADY'S MANTLE

Every morning, you will find dewdrops strung along the edges of this plant's seven-pointed leaves like a pearl necklace. The plants sparkle like diamonds in the sun. The drops used to be called "celestial water", and they were thought to possess magical properties. Alchemists even tried to win gold from these glittering beads.

But even without these watery gems, this perennial is impressive for its foliage, while its small, yellow green flowers are rather inconspicuous. They are gathered in clusters and are only a little lighter in colour than the leaves. Lady's mantle, a member of the rose family, likes fresh to moist soil, but will also thrive on dry and stony ground. It needs little care.

The alpine variety most common in Europe has leaves that are dark green on the top with a hairy, silvery underside. It can grow up to 30 cm (12 in) tall. You can also find shorter varieties; some lady's mantle only reaches 10 cm (4 in).

ROCK CRESS

Rock cress is a perennial that grows as low ground cover, forming a cushion on the earth. It produces numerous white or reddish to red flowers (or more rarely, yellow) between March and May. Its outstanding ability to grow on drystone walls makes it a perfect candidate for rock gardens. It also provides decorative borders for beds and gravel paths. Rock cress will do nicely in any garden soil provided there is good drainage; it doesn't like too much moisture and can even die in winter if water does not drain off well. It thrives in sunny locations, emerging from rock crevices or growing among rubble, rewarding the gardener with an almost overwhelming abundance of flowers in dense clusters. Its dentate leaves are covered in a grey felt.

BELLFLOWER

A large group of garden plants belongs to the bellflower family. As you might guess, these versatile plants owe their name to their bell-shaped blooms. They are a central feature in many rock gardens, and they are also quite popular as houseplants. The low varieties look particularly good growing among stones, just as they do in the mountains.
Campanula raineri, an especially fine Italian bellflower from the southern side of the Alps, is a diminutive beauty. It forms a loose mat about 10 cm (4 in) high. When its light blue flowers emerge in August and September, they seem enormous in comparison to the slender stems. It needs a sunny location with chalky soil.
The same applies to the tussock bellflower, which with its height of 30 cm (12 in) is much taller. It produces bluish violet flowers from June to August. The variety 'Karpaten-Krone' has silvery blue flowers, and 'Blue Dwarf' pure blue ones.

SEA PINK

This name can be botanically misleading, as sea pinks don't really have anything to do with the pink family. With its some 50 species, the sea pink or sea thrift actually belongs to the leadwort family and originates in the Mediterranean region. Some sorts come from the Near East and the Andes. These pretty, low-maintenance plants commonly grow as low cushions. They have thin, grass-like leaves and develop fairly tall stems with white to pink flowers that wave in the wind. The alpine thrift is the one most suitable for your rock garden. Its bushy foliage provides a nice background for the deep pink flowers, which rise up on stalks as high as 15 cm (6 in). A sunny location and soil with excellent drainage will help the sea pink thrive.

HOUSELEEK

The evergreen, hardy houseleek is also known as roof houseleek. Charlemagne is said to have advised his subjects to put this rosette-shaped plant on their roofs to ward off lightening. This superstition has long since gone out of vogue, but the juicy, fleshy leaves of some varieties of houseleek continue to play a role in folk medicine: they are said to have a beneficial effect on eye complaints and earache. Houseleeks are undemanding mountain dwellers and grow from rock crevices and in rubble. They thus do very well on walls and roofs and even in small stony hollows in rock gardens.

Around 40 varieties of houseleek are known, and there are practically countless cultivars and hybrids. Particularly suited to rock gardens are those varieties that are descendants of the mountain houseleek, which form 5-cm (2-in) rosettes composed of green, lance-like leaves. The stems, which can be as long as 20 cm (8 in), bear up to ten flowers, which are much frequented by bees. The flowering rosettes die off after first forming offsets to ensure propagation.

IRIS

The iris, also known as the sword lily, can play a double role in rock gardens. It can be planted in rocky flower beds, or it can be used to form a border around garden ponds.

This perennial, which is very popular as a cut flower, can lay claim to approximately 200 wild varieties and countless cultivars. It grows from a rhizome or a bulb. Its striking flower consists of three broad bracts, most often hanging downwards, and three narrower, upright inner petals.

The bulb iris blooms early in the year, while irises that grow from rhizomes come into flower later. The latter are also hardy. The rhizome varieties include the classic *Iris Germanica*, which produces small, bearded flowers of a rich purple shade during the late spring.

Irises can grow to a height of up to 80 cm (30 in), and are a valuable addition to your rock-garden landscape. Of course, there are any number of smaller varieties, like the crested iris. Some dwarf iris varieties grow only 6 cm (2$\frac{1}{2}$ in) tall. The iris likes slightly moist, chalky soil. Only the types suggested as pond-edge plants will thrive in very wet conditions. Growing iris requires some degree of patience, as plants sometimes have to get used to a location first and only achieve their full splendour after four years.

PASQUE FLOWER

Meadow anemone, crowfoot and windflower are other names for this popular harbinger of spring, presented here under its most common appellation, pasque flower. This perennial likes to grow in the sun or partial shade on permeable, chalky soil. It produces its bright, large flowers as early as March. Those growing in the wild are a protected species in many places, because their tendency to bloom early tempts people to pick them or even to dig them out and replant them in their own garden.

Pasque flowers have a rhizome that goes down deep into the soil. From it grow long stalks bearing mostly pinnate leaves that remain green in winter. The striking flowers are on hairy stalks and often droop. There are all kinds of different varieties. Every height and a wide range of colours are represented.

For example, the alpine pasque flower grows up to 50 cm (20 in) tall and produces white petals up to 6 cm (2½ in) in size. They are blue, purple or reddish on the outside and have a thick

covering of hairs. The spring pasque flower reaches a height of just 15 cm (6 in). It has white flowers that are bluish on the outside with beautiful golden-brown hairs.

LIVERLEAF

In contrast to most species, the liverleaf prefers shady spots and fresh, humusy soil. Like its relation, the pasque flower, it's a herald of spring, but a small one that barely reaches 15 cm (6 in). Its flowers range from blue to purple, pink or (rarely) white. In the wild, one may encounter liverleaf on lime-rich soil in the woods, where they are found in groups. This perennial gets its perhaps less than appealing name from its liver-shaped leaves: this is also one reason medieval healers used this plant to treat liver disorders. The prevailing idea at the time,

called the doctrine of signature, was that plants resembling an organ of the body would cure disease in that organ.

Full-flowered species are to be recommended, such as the *Hepatica transsilvanica*, which blooms very early in the year, even in late winter. Liverleaf is useful for adding colour to shady parts of the rock garden where other plants don't thrive. Liverleaf should never be removed from the wild where they occur, not only to preserve the beauty of a wild place, but also because they may be protected in some areas.

BITING STONECROP

Undemanding plants that grow well even under extreme circumstances are of course most welcome in rock gardens. Biting stonecrop or wall pepper is one such plant. It comes in several varieties and includes perennials and semi-shrubs.

Being a succulent plant, it can tolerate long periods of dryness, which is why it is often planted on roofs and walls along with the houseleek. This is probably the origin of the name wall pepper.

Most varieties of stonecrop, which originally came from North Africa, are small, ground covering perennials that form cushions. They are very hardy succulents that also look good in hanging pots. Biting stonecrop bears star-shaped yellow or reddish flowers that occur either singly or in clusters.

The toughness of this plant is demonstrated by the fact that it is often found growing on railway embankments and amid rubble. This is ample indication of its suitability for rock gardens.

Most varieties form a low mat, but there are some cultivars that grow to a height of up to 60 cm (24 in).

POPPY

A gardener's main reason for planting poppies in their garden is often a desire to add some intense colour to it. The flowers of the nearly 100 poppy varieties and countless cultivars bring more vivid colours to the garden than almost any other type of plant.

Many gardeners are content to put in annual varieties so they can sow them in different places every year. Perennial poppies prefer to remain in one location. These perennial varieties include the alpine poppy, which has pinnate leaves that form a rosette on the ground. Yellow or white cup-shaped flowers nod atop their slender stems. The

Iceland poppy is also available in yellow. It is one of the most suitable varieties for a rock garden. It blooms gaily in white, yellow and orange and grows only 20 cm (8 in) tall.

Most species and varieties of poppy grow best in locations where they will receive a great deal of sun. The perennials are, of course, more particular about soil conditions than the annuals. The smaller alpine perennials grow well in permeable chalky soil and therefore manage best in rock gardens.

If possible, you should reserve a whole section just for poppies; this produces a splendid sight in summer.

PHLOX

Phlox is a Greek word meaning "flame-coloured plant", which says a lot about this perennial.

The varieties that are most popular in Britain come from North America and appeared in European gardens at the start of the nineteenth century. Breeders have brought about some true floral miracles in the case of this amazingly adaptable plant. There are now varieties that are suitable for every taste and every purpose, including planting in rock gardens. Perhaps its versatility stems from the fact that it belongs to the Jacob's ladder family; a connection to heaven seems very suitable for such a heavenly plant. There are tiny kinds of phlox able to fill

any nooks and crannies in very small rock gardens, but phlox also occurs as an imposing perennial that provides a splendid floral background.

The lowest-growing variety is carpet phlox, which reaches a height of 20 cm (8 in), often even less. It quickly forms spreading mats that are eminently suitable for difficult slopes and drystone walls. These should be regularly watered, though. In April and May, it produces a surprising abundance of flowers in all the colours your heart could desire. The tried-and-true 'G. F. Wilson' cultivar, with its slate-blue flowers, is to be recommended.

PRIMROSE

The Latin name of this flower, *primula*, means "little first one". As this suggests, the flowers of this small plant are some of the first to appear very early in the year. Another name for it is key flower, because its flowers occur in clusters that resemble keys on a key ring.

Primroses are usually perennial herbs with a forked rhizome. It ends each growing season as a flowering shoot and sprouts again from a side bud.

The primrose's mountain origins make it eminently suitable for rock gardens, as does its small size coupled with great floral productivity. The simple, often dentate leaves contrast nicely with the colourful petals of the bell-shaped or plate-shaped flowers, which emerge from green sepals.

Native wild varieties of primrose are protected. However, a wide range of cultivars is available. If you tell your garden centre exactly what you want the primrose for, they will likely be able to recommend a "tailor-made" variety. All primroses like fairly moist soil while they are growing, but too much moisture in winter is not good for them. They prefer relatively humid conditions and partial shade.

A note of caution: lovely though they are, working with primroses can be problematic, as many people develop an allergy to the primine produced by their leaves and stems.

SUN ROSE

The sun rose thrives in chalky, sandy, permeable soil, which is just the kind of soil usually found in rock gardens.

As its name suggests, the sun rose prefers locations where it will receive plenty of sunlight and blooms primarily in summer. In addition, the yellow, orange, red or white flowers also look like little suns. Its abundant flowers and small size make the sun rose a must in any rock garden.

Almost all of the more than 100 known varieties are low-growing plants that only reach between 10 and 20 cm (4–8 in) in height. Their flowers occur in clusters. A very small selection of the available sorts demonstrates the astonishing variety amongst these pretty little plants:

The 'Fireball' blooms a luxuriant dark red, as does the variety 'Supreme'; 'Cerise Queen' produces pink, full flowers; 'The Bride', on the other hand, has white flowers; the flowers of 'Lawrenson's pink' have a light centre surrounded by pale pink petals.

Sun roses are an enchanting sight in front of walls or along bordering paths and flower beds. If they are well sheltered in winter and situated in a sunny spot, these plants will give you lasting pleasure.

SAXIFRAGE

Many kinds of saxifrage are available to gardeners in the U.K. This perennial originated in high mountainous regions. Some species are protected. The Latin name for this plant, *Saxifragus*, means "stone breaking", which suggests how ideal it is for rock gardens. It received its name because it likes to grow out of earth-filled crevices in rocks. Saxifrage prefers sun or partial shade. Mossy saxifrage is a rosette-like creeping plant that grows 10 to 20 cm (4–8 in) tall and forms a white mat of flowers in May or June. There are also some taller cultivars in other colours that produce slightly larger flowers. Purple saxifrage grows even lower to the ground. If you plant it in a cool, moist location it will reward you in early spring with lovely purple-red flowers.

ALYSSUM

Alyssum, also known as Alison or sweet alyssum, is ideal for small walls and borders in rock gardens. It is a mostly yellow-flowering cruciferous plant. It originated in the Mediterranean region and thus prefers sunny spots in the garden with permeable, relatively poor soil. It should be fertilised very sparingly to prevent the leaves taking over at the expense of the flowers.

The silvery-grey foliage fits well into a rock garden and forms a restrained background for the bright, intense flower clusters. The most frequent variety in Europe is mountain alyssum, which grows to 20 cm (8 in) in height, producing grey-green foliage before yellow blossoms appear between April and June. Golden alyssum, also known as *Aurina saxatilis*, has similar golden flowers, but grows somewhat taller and has been developed into some lovely cultivars. 'Gold Dust' is one example; it has dark yellow, full flowers and is a splendid plant for edging paved paths and borders.

CRANESBILL (GERANIUM)

Because of its botanical name, *Geranium*, cranesbill is often confused with the popular balcony plant, pelargonium. There is also a slight similarity between the leaves and flowers of the two plants. The flowers, which are flat and coloured pink to violet, possess a similar charm. However, cranesbill is almost always used for completely different purposes than the sensitive pelargonium, and often serves as ground cover in rock gardens.

One species, the *Geranium cinereum*, which comes to us from Italy, grows to about 15 cm (6 in). It has dark-edged, bright pink flowers and very pretty leaves with a grey, hairy underside.

Cultivars of this perennial spread from 12 to 30 cm (5–12 in) wide and are therefore a good choice for covering coarse gravel and small rocks. The hybrid 'Ballerina' is highly recommended. It grows 12 to 15 cm (5–6 in) tall and produces purple flowers throughout the summer.

One species native to most of Europe is meadow cranesbill, which will fit well into your rock garden if you have a pond or stream there. This thirsty perennial will thrive on their banks, flowering from May to August. The flowers are a splendid blue-violet, and the leaves are divided into seven parts with deeply cut lobes.

SPURGE

The spurge family contains many species. They all prefer permeable, sandy-loamy, relatively dry, humusy soil. They are also known as euphorbia, after an ancient Greek physician. Spurge is a succulent plant that likes sun. There are several sorts that are extremely suitable for rock gardens. These perennials are mostly low growing, with blue-green foliage and produce rich yellowy or orange-coloured flowers. They all contain a more or less poisonous milky sap.

Spurges play the same role in Europe as cactuses do in North America, and they can be treated along the same lines. Like their fellows in the New World, they tolerate dryness well and are thus ideal for rock gardens. Some species have a reputation for keeping moles and voles at bay, another trait that many gardeners will appreciate. Creeping spurge is one popular variety; it has fleshy, blue-green, oval to spatulate leaves that it keeps throughout the winter.

Euphorbia griffithi 'Fireglow' is very tolerant and will grow well in almost any location on any soil. This tall bushy plant grows to about 90 cm (3 ft) in height. The fiery, brick red flowers are only one of its many attractions. Dark green leaves with a reddish mid-vein lend drama to the garden all season long. It also makes a strong display in autumn.

GRASSES AND FERNS IN ROCK GARDENS

It is never advisable to gather decorative grasses and ferns for your rock garden during walks in the woods. Quite apart from the damage you will do to the countryside, most wild plants will not live up to your expectations in the garden. But you will find plants for every need and circumstance at a garden centre.

Green or even brown varieties of grass brighten up every rock garden, not just in summer, but also in the bleaker months. The huge variety includes types that form low cushions and others that grow high above our heads. As a rule, smaller species are more suitable for rock gardens. They grow under shrubs and trees, enliven shady spots along walls and can be used as a contrast to colourful flowers. They give the garden a more natural appearance.

In the rock garden, ornamental grasses play a leading role. They serve to soften contours and form waving tufts. Once they have taken root, they can remain in the same location year in, year out. They look better and better the longer they are there, and barely need any maintenance. Because of their relatively permanent nature, it is advisable to decide where you want grasses when first establishing the garden, if possible.

In contrast to grasses, most ferns tend to like shade, although there are some cultivars that can take sun. The ferns available for purchase are already adapted to the needs of your garden and are thus preferable to wild plants.

They should be planted in spring. The soil underneath trees or shrubs is particularly good. If this kind of soil is not available, prepare the spot where you intend to plant them, mixing in peat and rotted leaves or needles to improve permeability of the soil. Woodruff, great bellflowers, violets, lilies-of-the-valley, asarabacca and lungwort all look attractive near ferns. The exotic character of ferns is particularly emphasised when their fronds emerge from amongst low, cushion-like perennials. Naturally, almost all the plants mentioned in the following section have as many uses outside the rock garden as within it.

CHINESE SILVER GRASS

Because a rock garden is a relatively dry biotope, some kind of water feature nearby provides a nice contrast, and Chinese silver grass is an ideal plant to position near water. This slender grass with its striking inflorescences is a lovely sight right into winter. It also looks very attractive in large vases; it does not mind being cut.

It is important to plant Chinese silver grass in deep, permeable soil. Most species like slightly moist soil and appreciate sun. Some varieties spread rapidly and are thus good for reinforc-ing the sides of ponds and embankments. The plants can be easily propagated by division.

The Japanese variety of this plant reaches an impressive height of 3 metres (10 ft) and forms dense clusters with arching leaves. But nobody has to do without silver grass, because there are cultivars of various heights and also with various patterning on their leaves. The smallest sorts grow to be 80 cm to 1 metre (30 in to 3 ft) tall. In autumn, most of these grasses turn brown-red and by their colouring almost take on the appearance of flowers.

FOUNTAIN GRASS

You can grow perennial fountain grass in full sun on normal garden soil. It forms clusters and looks simply wonderful waving its plushy fruit clusters in the wind.

The stalks with their soft, bottlebrush-like spikelets are also a valuable addition to bouquets and dried-flower arrangements. These spikelets are what gave the plant its other name, swamp foxtail. The cultivars stem from the approximately 50 species native to East Asia and Australia.

A few varieties of these grasses even develop hard stalks as they develop over the years. They grow to a height of between 40 and 80 cm (15–30 in). Their leaves arch gracefully and thus soften contours in a rocky landscape. The attractive flower stalks develop in late summer and the plants keep their woolly fruits right into winter. This is another good reason to have this plant in your garden.

The lowest-growing sorts of fountain grass, standing about 40 cm (15 in) high, are 'Japonicum', which forms sparse tufts and has white tips on its flowers, and 'Weserbergland', with a low, fanned-out shape.

You should give these attractive plants a location that is sheltered from the wind so that the stems do not break. The soil should be relatively rich and consistently kept slightly moist. To propagate this plant, divide it in spring. Some sorts of fountain grass can be sown at this time and grown under glass before planting them outside in May.

HART'S TONGUE FERN

This fern received its rather unique name because the long, somewhat pointed shape of its leaves resembles that of a deer's tongue. It grows especially well along old walls, under trees and anywhere else it finds moist and chalky soil. Hart's tongue fern is a member of the spleenwort family and is amenable to cooler conditions. Almost all of these ferns are evergreens, so their slender leaves will add a nice touch of green to any rock garden throughout the entire year. Some varieties also sport very nice large, tufted crests on the tips of their leaves. However, all of them grow in clumps on the ground like lettuces and, with their large leaves, form noticeable patches of green even in the shaded locations they prefer.

The hart's-tongue fern can be propagated by sowing in summer or—in the case of cultivars—by dividing the plants. Offshoots can also be grown from leaf stalks, which quickly take root when placed about 1 cm ($\frac{1}{2}$ in) deep in appropriate potting soil.

VELVET GRASS

Velvet grass likes fresh, humusy or even boggy soil (such as that found near a pond). As its name suggests, it is a member of the grass family, *Poaceae*. This plant is a native and very widespread. It grows on loamy and sandy soil under moist or even wet conditions. Loose, humusrich sandy to marshy soil are what velvet grass likes best.

In the countryside, velvet grass mostly grows in clumps in pastures, but in spite of it's appealing name cows and sheep refuse to eat it. Animals will not even touch hay that contains velvet grass. Gardeners used to regard velvet grass as a weed before they discovered the decorative characteristics of this plant, which grows to a height of 30 cm to 1 metre (1–3 ft).

The attraction of velvet grass in the garden stems from its woolly appearance and the soft hairs on its stalk and leaves. Many species form tough, creeping rhizomes that are extremely durable. As a result, you are well advised to consider carefully before planting this grass in your garden, for if you should one day decide you don't want it anymore, it will take quite a lot of hoeing and chopping to get rid of it again.

ORCHARD GRASS

Orchard grass is encountered on the edges of paths and in sparse woods, on fields and meadows. It is a member of the sweet grass family and occurs everywhere in the temperate zone. It likes sunny or partially shaded locations and fresh soil. Plant breeders have devoted much attention to this grass, developing varieties that are important as pasture plants and for making hay.

Some of the cultivated varieties are also interesting for the gardener. For example, there is ribbon grass with its relatively broad, yellowish or white striped leaves. It looks most attractive when combined with low-growing perennials and other grasses with bluish or dark green leaves. Orchard grass is not very demanding and, under optimal conditions, it can grow to almost 1.5 metres (5 ft) in height. Its small heads are gathered closely together in slightly bluish or violet-coloured panicles.

In rock gardens, orchard grass is useful if you are trying to create a natural effect. As in the woods, it serves as an attractive undergrowth for trees and shrubs and also provides flower beds with an elegantly waving border.

SCALE FERN

In contrast to many other ferns, scale fern tolerates some light and moderate warmth. This does not mean, however, that it should be considered a real sun lover. In ancient times, scale fern was prized as a medicinal plant. It generally grows only 10 to 20 cm (4–8 in) tall, making it a good candidate for small gardens. It can be planted like an herb between fairly large stones and near drystone walls. It also likes to grow in troughs and in joints between bricks. The scale fern grows fast.

This fern's somewhat leathery leaves are not as finely pinnate as those of many larger ferns. They grow from the stalk like little elliptical ears, forming small fronds. The leaves are a dull green on top and silvery green and shiny underneath. They remain green during winter. As the scale fern needs warmth, it requires some protection in winter, unless it is situated in a completely sheltered location near to the walls of a house, which will give off some heat.

If the scale fern is to be healthy and develop its intense green colour, it must be planted in lime-rich soil. You can propagate the plant by sowing its spores or dividing it, depending on how much you want for your garden. As a rule, it will be easier to obtain plants from your garden centre.

PAMPAS GRASS

Pampas grass, a native of South America and New Zealand, is not for every small garden, as it does need plenty of room. The original species grows up to 3 metres (10 ft) tall, so many gardeners may find it takes too much space. But there is a cultivar, 'Pumila', that only grows 1 metre (3 ft) tall and thus could fit in a moderately large rock garden. This grass looks best growing alone as a tall clump in a sunny location on rich soil.

The main charm of this large plant comes from the clusters of blossoms that emerge from bunches of narrow, sharp-edged leaves in summertime. Their feathery tufts are visible from afar as they wave in the wind.

If you want to enjoy these striking plumes in winter as well, you can cut them in spring and prepare them for dry flower arrangements. The variety 'Rosea' is particularly distinctive. As its name indicates, its flower clusters have a slightly reddish hue.

Pampas grass will be grateful for a sheltered, dry location. During long dry periods, observe it to see whether it needs a little water. In the growing season, it can use an occasional dose of fertiliser. Being a sun lover, pampas grass needs shelter in winter. This is best done by covering it with straw or spruce branches and placing plenty of fallen leaves around its base.

SPLEENWORT

One sort of spleenwort, the hart's tongue fern, has already been introduced (see page 68). The other types are also characterised by their extreme leafiness. Some species even grow in tropical trees. But as temperate zone gardeners, we are more interested in those varieties that stay on the ground. Spleenworts get their name from the fact that they were once considered to have medicinal value in the treatment of spleen complaints.

One type that has found its way into gardens is black spleenwort, so called because of the colour of its leaf stalks. It does not like chalky soil, but it does like warmth, which is why it needs a sheltered location. Its relative, wall rue, also likes relatively warm temperatures, but grows well in a lime-rich soil. Wall rue grows from just 3 to 15 cm (1–6 in) tall, so it is a fern of choice where space is lacking.

Forked spleenwort, as its name suggests, has interesting leaves which are divided into two or three parts. It is difficult to recognise as one of the fern family, as it resembles a hanging clump of grass. Maidenhair spleenwort is undemanding and exists in two varieties, one that doesn't like chalky soil, and one that is grateful for it.

POLYPODY

Polypodies, whose name is taken from the Greek word for "many feet", are so called because of the appearance of their creeping rootstock. They occur all over the world, growing on other plants or from rock crevices. They prefer shade and high humidity. You will also find polypodies in British woods.

As it is a popular indoor and outdoor plant, cultivators have naturally given it their attention, developing varieties that are suitable for rock gardens. At first glance, these seem no different than the polypodies that grow wild. But they do produce more leaves and are more tolerant of garden conditions than their fellows in the woods. Like their wild cousins, cultivated polypodies have a characteristic rhizome that creeps underground and is extremely sweet. This is why the native variety has been given the name sweet fern or wood liquorice. It is no wonder that healers praised the curative properties of the root of the polypody even in ancient times. It contains all sorts of tannins, fats and oils that continue to play a role in natural medicine to this day.

In the garden, these feathery, evergreen plants are mostly used for decorative purposes in locations that other plants are not so keen on. Polypodies grow to a height of 30 to 40 cm (12–15 in) and have an upright form.

COMMON MALE FERN OR SHIELD FERN

The dried roots or extracts from the rhizome of this evergreen plant were, and still are, used in natural healing as a remedy to treat tapeworms. Its spores do not develop into new ferns straightaway, but first form a shoot that looks like a small, fat worm.

Various cultivars are available at garden centres. They all grow from around 50 cm to 1 metre (20 in–3 ft) tall. Plants of this group suitable for different tastes and garden conditions abound. For example, the golden-scaled male fern bears glossy, dark-green leaves on stalks covered with brown scales. There is also the crested shield fern, which should be planted directly at the edge of ponds because it appreciates boggy, damp locations. The cultivar known as autumn fern has red spores, and the tips of its fronds are also red when it is young.

The best-known variety is the common male fern, which will grow well without tree protection in sunny locations if there is enough moisture in the soil. Shelter it with spruce boughs in the winter.

Despite its decorative form, this species' interest in the garden is limited by the fact that it is not green in winter. Low-growing varieties of alpine origin that need no protection in winter are more popular.

COLOUR IN ROCK GARDENS

Even if some evergreen plants have weathered the winter with us, providing the rock garden with colour and contour, after all those grey months the eye longs for more intense colours. The brightly coloured flowers of bulbs proclaim the news that spring has finally arrived.

A vibrant flower medley composed of aubrietia, tulips and narcissus gives any rock garden refreshing colour accents.

Snowdrops are the earliest flowers to appear in the new year, but they are by no means a sure sign that winter is behind us. Not until the crocuses and then the larger tulips dare to put their heads above ground can one say that the frosty season will soon be at an end, if it isn't already.

Narcissuses join them, and irises and grape hyacinths follow not long thereafter. The predominantly greyish hue of the garden begins to yield to a blaze of colour. Finally, cushions of aubrietia come along to soften any remaining stony contours.

But the plant of the season is definitely the tulip. Its many forms provide a huge variety of colourful highlights. Tulip breeders have given the Dutch national flower every imaginable colour. They have also developed tulips with crinkled petals and peony flowers, small varieties such as the dasystemon tulip, and others with stately stems and enormous blooms such as the Darwin tulip, which grows up to 70 cm (27 in) tall.

What is more, the queen of spring no longer rules for only a few weeks—these days, the late blooming tulips that have become available don't give way to summer flowers until very late in the season.

Tulip bulbs should be planted in groups in the sandy, humusy soil of rock gardens between September and November. You should ensure that water drains well from the location. If necessary, put in additional drainage. Please note: carefully mark the spots where you have planted bulbs so that no one goes to work there later with a hoe or spade.

These robust plants need winter protection only in the first year after they have been planted; covering them with branches is the best method. It is still more important to protect them against voles, for which tulip bulbs are a delicacy. Chemicals are mostly only a temporary help against the hungry creatures, and can cause damage in other ways. Tight wire mesh is much better; the voles cannot get through it, but it poses no obstacle for the roots of the bulbs. You can also buy special plastic baskets for this purpose.

Happily, caring for tulips is relatively easy. All that is really necessary is to apply fertiliser

before and after their flowering period. It is also important to remove any wilted flowers, cutting high up so that the stem is not damaged. The leaves should only be removed after they have dried out and turned yellow. Until then, the leaves are actually still very productive, providing nutrients for the next bloom cycle.

Patches of colour that seem to sprout out of crevices make rock gardens a true feast for the eyes.

The greyness of the seemingly immutable stone and the colourful splendour of the flowers create a particularly lovely contrast each spring.

VEGETABLE
GARDENS

THE RIGHT SOIL

It would be going too far to claim that the well-being of plants depends solely on what their roots take from the soil—there are all sorts of other factors that also play a role—but soil and nutrients do play the key role. There are a number of things you can do to make sure the soil in your garden is the best it can be.

If you want abundant harvests, the soil in your vegetable garden needs a lot of care. This includes watering, fertilising and loosening it to increase its permeability. A good harvest, of particularly nice pumpkins, for example, will reward your efforts.

Normally soil renews itself on its own. Everything that grows in it dies off, is turned into humus by the creatures living in it and serves as food for the next plants to come. But when we harvest plants, we take away some of the nutrients from the soil every growing season. If we don't want harvests to diminish, we must compensate for what is removed by improving the soil, by adding compost or with other measures.

When soil is used for gardening, it also becomes more tightly packed and thus less permeable. You must counter this, as permeability has a great influence on the growth of plants grow and the success of the harvest. It should be increased by mechanical means and by adding organic matter to the soil.

Only in a few cases will it be necessary to carry out an expensive soil analysis. You can judge for yourself if all is well by observing your plants' growth. There are also kits widely available to test how acid or alkaline the soil is. Excessive fertilisation is not a cure for all ills; on the contrary, moderation is the key.

Soil that does not contain enough nutrients requires compost and green manuring. Green manuring means sowing low, fast-growing, green plants before, during or, best of all, after the harvest. They die off in winter and are worked into the soil in spring. These green plants—such as field peas, lupines, mustard or fodder radishes—can also be dug in while still green. Leftovers from the harvest such as the leaves of

vides an even wider range of nutrients than green manure.

In addition to adding nutrients, green manure and compost improve soil permeability. Soil needs to be turned and loosened mechanically, with the proper tools, but it should only be turned rarely, because this mixes up the different layers of soil and disturbs the organisms living there. Generally it suffices to loosen the surface with a single-prong cultivator.

Watering is an active way of preventing dry soil, but you can also do this passively by mulching. Mulching means covering the soil with plant remains (such as grass clippings—though watch out for grass growing later where you put them), half-rotted compost or leaves. It also prevents undesirable plants from growing, especially under shrubs and trees. The extent of watering should always take into account the type of plant, its location and the season, as well as other factors. Here again, too much is just as harmful as too little. You will soon learn the right amount.

some vegetables can be used as green manure as well. They form humus, which should be added in the form of compost, because it pro-

Mulching—covering the soil with a mixture of plant remains, half-rotted compost, leaves, or straw—prevents the soil from becoming too dry (left).

How much you should water depends on a number of factors. The best way to find out is simply to try and see what works best!

WEEDS

In the age of organic gardening, the word "weed" has fallen from favour – and a good thing, too. In using it here, we only want to say that you can utilise natural methods to combat plant intruders that could damage your garden. Herbicides should only be used as an emergency solution.

> Weeding is inevitable, but it should be done in moderation. Only declare battle against undesired plants when they endanger the productivity of your vegetable garden—and then do it properly and thoroughly.

Let us emphasise it once more: only plants that truly endanger the productivity of your vegetable garden should be seen as weeds and combated accordingly. A few wild plants growing in unused corners of a small garden do no harm at all; in fact, many a stinging nettle can give us pleasure by providing food for caterpillars of the butterflies that enchant us so much. But if paved areas are being destroyed by plants growing in the joints or are made too slippery in wet conditions, something has to be done.

We don't like to see such plants in lawns, either, because here they are rivals for nutrients. This is even more of an issue in vegetable beds—in the worst case they can even crowd out the sown or planted vegetables. So it's important to get weeds under control before they can get established, let alone take over. April or May is the best time to start weed control. You have to distinguish between two sorts of undesirable plants: short-lived and annual weeds require a different approach than perennial ones. The short-lived and annual plants can be dealt with in the same way. Although they soon die, their seeds can make them a persistent problem. You must take action with a hoe before they come into bloom. Whether grass or poppy—the root dies off if you simply chop off the plant.

Y ou can be even more certain that the plant will die if you use a sharp hoe to cut off the plant stalk just above or even slightly under the surface of the soil. You can use a combined hoe and fork (a clever tool which has a hoe blade on one side and a fork with three tines on the other), a pull hoe or an oscillating hoe. You will be particularly successful in warm weather, because the cuts in the plants and the chopped-off sections will dry quickly.

Perennial weeds die off every year above ground, but come back again with unremitting malice. Bindweed, couch grass, buttercups, gallant soldier and field horsetail are particularly obstinate. You have no choice but to dig them out, roots and all, because each and every small part of the root that remains in the soil will produce new shoots. And you should never put any of these pests in your compost bin, but instead burn them or put them in the rubbish.

While stinging nettles can be torn out of the ground at one jerk with all their roots, finding all the roots of couch grass can become an endeavour of almost archaeological dimensions. Never give up, because otherwise this greedy plant is sure to return. The best time to weed it out is after rain, as the roots will be less tenacious, making it possible to pull out metre-long strands.

VEGETABLES FROM YOUR OWN GARDEN

People who grow vegetables in their own garden are sometimes scoffed at, although many would admit that this kind of effort is well worthwhile even if it isn't economical. If your main incentive is to save money on produce, a vegetable garden isn't for you. The personal gains of having a vegetable patch are something else entirely.

One of the things money cannot buy: homegrown vegetables give you a sense of achievement and can't be beaten for freshness. Lettuces in all their variety are particularly gratifying, grow fast and don't need room. Above are the varieties Lollo rosso and Lollo bianco.

Most home gardeners don't grow their crops for profit. And though the benefits of physical exercise in the outdoors is well known, most do not pursue vegetable gardening for the workout. The incomparable satisfaction of growing your own food is one of the joys of the garden. In addition, in these days of chemical and pesticide use in commercial farming, home vegetable gardeners know exactly what goes on their tables—which is more than those of us who buy from the shops can often say. What is more, if you take the effort to plant your own vegetables, you will enjoy what you've harvested in a completely different way than people who buy produce, let alone those who live on tinned and preserved food. A gardener is thrilled when the various vitamin-filled delicacies ripen, for fresh-picked produce tastes "the way it used to taste". If you were once someone who lived from tins, you will probably see vegetables as an uninteresting side dish. Straight from the garden they are a delicacy, a meal in and of themselves, or wonderful partners to meat or fish.

Let us begin with salads. In shops they don't always look so fresh, even though freshness is vital to their full enjoyment. Harvested just before eating they are fresh; indeed, nothing could be fresher. And if the soil

Salad vegetables, including tomatoes, need regular watering as they grow very fast. This makes them good for filling gaps between vegetables that grow slowly. Radishes, for instance, will be harvested long before the other plants expand and need the space they have occupied.

Much the same goes for lettuces planted between young cabbage plants: they will be picked before the cabbages spread their leaves. One little-appreciated advantage of lettuces should be mentioned here: their rapid growth makes them prime candidates for children's gardens, as children are impatient and want to see quickly what becomes of the seeds they have sown. Lettuces soon become visible above the soil and mature so quickly that children won't lose interest. In addition, lettuces are easy to harvest and can be prepared for the table with little effort. Success thus comes in a relatively short space of time, encouraging children to take on more difficult plants. Lettuces also grow well in boxes on the balcony or window ledge. The many types of cutting

is right, they will taste far better than any you can buy. The perfect soil should be slightly acidic (pH 6.5), friable and worked through with organic materials. A sunny location is desirable.

Tomatoes (left) need a sunny, warm location and plenty of fertiliser. They are harvested from July to the end of October.

Carrots (below) are particularly rich in vitamins and nutrients. Their main requirement is loose soil.

lettuce that don't need much room and grow back again are to be recommended for small gardens. Here are a few gourmet tips for leafy salad vegetables that you won't find in shops, or at least not in this form: dandelion leaves can be blanched and eaten if they are picked just after they have sprouted, while they are still very light green in colour; nasturtiums or rocket salad will add a bit of "bite" to your salad; and winter cress has a similarly pungent taste. You can buy corn salad or lamb's lettuce in shops, but it is usually not very crisp—at least not as crisp as if it had come from your garden. You can pick celery stalks fresh from the garden right up into winter.

Another important category of vegetables is the cabbage family. It is normally divided into three large groups: leafy cabbages, of which the best-known member is probably kale; cabbages with expanded, bulbous stems, which include the various sorts of kohlrabi; and cabbages with flowers or thickened flower stalks, such as cauliflower. All of them have their strengths as regards taste, from the tanginess of kale after the first frost and the elegance of white cabbage, which tastes best *al dente*, to broccoli with its asparagus-like flavour. One tip for growing cabbage: if you plant celery nearby it may prevent the cabbage from being attacked by the caterpillars of the cabbage white butterfly.

Pulses are a valuable addition to salads or are often used as salads on their own. Beans are particularly good, especially when served with onions, leeks or shallots. And even fairly small beds in your garden will produce sufficient amounts of both. How about covering your fence with climbing runner beans? They are a treat for the eyes and supply vegetables at the same time. Leeks or

shallots intended for the same salad give off a pleasant aroma in the garden and have such an intense flavour that you don't need many plants.

The pumpkin family, *Curcurbitaceae*, is another large vegetable group. It includes melons, cucumbers, courgette and the various kinds of actual pumpkin. Notable among these are the giant pumpkins, fun to grow and a hit at agricultural fairs, but not so suitable for small gardens. Smaller types of pumpkin, some with decorative leaves, and the many small ornamental gourds are members of this family as well.

Courgette is particularly recommended for small gardens, because one plant is enough to supply a small family. The new mini-sized cultivars of many popular vegetables and lettuces that have been developed for small gardens are virtually tailor-made for small households.

COMPANION PLANTING

Cleverly planned, a vegetable garden can look almost as pretty as an ornamental one. Vegetables also produce flowers and different sorts complement one another both in colour and form. It is, however, important to know which plants get on well together and which do not. Then nothing stands in the way of creating an attractive mixture.

> Mixed beds offer many advantages. They are better defended against pests, nutrients in the soil are used more effectively, and your vegetable bed looks more interesting and lively. Here is an example with carrots and onions.

Nature shows us the way. If you observe carefully, you will soon be able to tell which plants get on well together and which ones prefer to avoid each other's company. Flowers and vegetables by no means need to be kept strictly apart. On the contrary, beds in which pretty annuals flower between the cabbages look especially appealing. It is partly this visual mixture that gives multi-purpose gardens their special charm.

However, there are some strange enmities, such as that between peas and tomatoes or between tomatoes and potatoes, even though they taste so good together in many dishes. It is more understandable that leeks and runner beans don't get on together, as they are of similar heights (the leeks always have the worst of it).

There are some even stranger friendships, however. For example, onions and strawberries grow extremely well together in one bed, even though they are completely different in taste.

Of course, how they taste to us is not terribly relevant here, but rather the mutual benefit they derive from being planted together.

It has not yet been completely explained why certain combinations of vegetables are better protected against pests than each sort growing on its own, but researchers suspect that scent and root "messages" are responsible. For example, you will find far fewer flea beetles in beds where lettuce and cabbage are growing together than in monocultures. The direct repellent effect of marigolds on nematodes (threadworms) has now been scientifically proved, and clever gardeners will deliberately plant marigolds in beds that contain plants particularly at risk, such as strawberries, peas, spinach or onions. You can combat thread-worms with poisons, called nematicides, but by using flowers instead you kill two birds with one stone: your beds look brighter and you can protect your crops without endangering yourself or your plants with strong poison. Silver beet surrounded by flowery decoration has a charm all its own.

Here is a short list of some harmonious combinations: tomatoes, cabbage and beetroot; garlic and strawberries; lettuce, spinach and Brussels sprouts; silver beet, carrots and lettuce; kohlrabi and salsify; sweet corn, cucumber and onions.

These few examples are by no means the only possibile combinations, and mixtures of flowers and vegetables—which are usually unproblematic with annuals—have not been mentioned. Lettuces are particularly sociable.

Even if the numerous possibilities for combinations are tempting, you won't get a good harvest unless the individual plants have enough room.

They grow well with every sort of herb, like to have onions, leeks, cucumbers or strawberries nearby, and welcome cabbage or peas in the same bed.

Companion planting has all sorts of other advantages for your garden, as well. Because the soil is continually in the shade of some plants' leaves during the growing season, it does not dry out as fast. The mixture of plants with deep and shallow roots means the range of nutrients in any one location is more efficiently utilised, and planting high and low plants together produces more visual variety. But all the same, avoid cramming everything together! If your vegetables do not have enough space, you may end up with an unnecessarily small harvest.

Something that is almost more important than the question of what plants grow well together is the order in which they are planted in a particular bed. This is called crop rotation. If you grow the same plants year after year in the same location, the soil becomes impoverished and more prone to pests and diseases. For this reason, it is important to follow certain rules when changing crops. The basic principle is to put in heavy feeders (tomatoes, cucumbers, members of the cabbage family) in the first year, in the second year medium feeders (lettuces, root vegetables), and in the third year light feeders that at the same time build up nitrogen in the soil. In the fourth year you should fertilise the soil again with fresh compost and the cycle can begin

What gets on with what? One sometimes sees unlikely bedfellows as far as taste is concerned: in this case, strawberries and onions side by side.

anew. If the soil is well cultivated and receives regular doses of well rotted compost, strict crop rotation like this is not absolutely necessary. As well as putting in compost, you can also use green manuring and increase the beneficial effect on the soil by planting combination crops.

Besides this yearly crop rotation, you should also keep in mind the order in which different vegetables mature during the same growing season. Gardeners speak of early, main and late crops and each should consist of plants that are not related, if possible. This is because there are pests that specialise in a particular sort of plant. If it is absent for a while, the pests either die from lack of food or go elsewhere.

Here is one example for a good order of crops: lamb's lettuce as a spring vegetable, cauliflower as the main crop, winter radish or spinach as a late harvest. Many main crops, however, are so long in maturing that they need the entire season. Some of these include salsify, chicory and kale.

Leeks and lettuces enjoy each other's company.

Silver beet, shown here with fennel, gets along well with almost every sort of vegetable and lettuce.

ORNAMENTAL
GARDENS

CHILDREN'S GARDENS

Many young families with children have a small garden at their disposal. This can give rise to a clash of interests: should the plot of land be a playground or a flowery paradise? But both ends can be achieved. However small your garden may be, you can cater to both the desire for fun and the desire for beauty.

Of course, the point of a children's garden is not to acquaint them with the hard work involved in gardening, because fun learning is just as important in the garden as elsewhere. By picking fruit themselves and living among colourful flowers, your children can develop a relationship to nature and the environment through play.

You won't be able to put in a football field or a plantation anyway, so compromise seems expedient: one part of the garden can be for playing and another for the grown-ups' flower beds. Both can be situated so that you can keep an eye on the children while you are gardening or resting in a summerhouse or on a lounge in some peaceful corner, and so that their toys and balls don't wind up in the flower beds too often.

Small children still don't need all that much scope for action and are happy with a sandpit and a little space on the patio. Older children will want a piece of lawn where they can at least play badminton or toss a frisbee. So the size of the children's area depends on their age, as does the way it is separated from the rest of the garden. For very small children, it is enough to have a few shrubs or a low hedge that can grow with the children. As the games get wilder, you can put up netting and other obstacles. If at all possible, it's nice to have some play equipment like swings or climbing frames. The more natural they look, the better:

Children need room to
play, so you should
provide plenty of it if you
want to avoid damage to
your part of the garden.

The best way for children
to learn to respect and
take an interest in the
variety of nature is by
experiencing their own
garden.

rustic-looking seesaws made of tree trunks, small log cabins, climbing bars or, best of all, a real climbing tree. The tree has to be able to take some rough treatment, but has an advantage over manmade equipment in that children can play on and in it more imaginatively.

Conifers are not suitable for this purpose, as they are prickly and leak resin, which is neither fun for the children nor good for their clothes. Linden trees, maples, beeches or alders are much better, but such large trees will probably be out of the question for very small gardens. For this reason, it is advisable to plant trees that are of lesser proportions. *Fagus sylvatica 'Tortuosa'*, the so-called "tortuous beech", for example, grows in bizarre, gnarled shapes but is not very tall—ideal for small gardens. And it provides room to build a tree house in one of its large forks.

Fruit trees also make very good climbing trees that are not too tall. Cherry trees, apple trees and pear trees are pleasing to look at whether in blossom or laden with fruit, grow to a moderate height and can take a lot of punishment. Of course, all that climbing won't exactly encourage their productivity, but it won't completely stop them producing either. This creates a twofold effect: the children can practise climbing and pick the fruit while doing so. Children who otherwise are growing up far

from nature will learn an important lesson: fruit doesn't grow in the supermarket and fruit you pick yourself tastes twice as good.

Children often go to work in a garden with great energy, so they deserve a break every so often!

This log cabin village made from tree trunks will be suitable only for more spacious small gardens, but it is a true paradise for children.

The second aspect of children's gardens is division of use. The adult' space and the children's play area should only be separated where their interests could collide.

Both may have activities in common—many lawn games, like boule, appeal to all ages, and children may take an interest in growing flowers or vegetables, or simply enjoy the sight and scent of the blooms. Of course, children should not be made to help with serious manual work in the garden right away, as it is sometimes very strenuous. But it is never too early for them to start with some of the easier gardening jobs.

In the previous chapter we saw how important it is for children to plant, tend and harvest in the garden. What was said about vegetable gardens applies equally to ornamental gardens. In fact, an ornamental garden is especially suitable because of the quick success it brings. A child who picks a bouquet from their own garden for Mother's Day or a birthday will be doubly proud to present the flowers to someone special. Nature can only really be understood through close contact with it, and this understanding is a very important step in children's exploration of

the world. At first they get to know the rhythms of day and night by watching the behaviour of the plants in their flower bed. They see the effects of weather and realise there are relationships between creatures like bees or butterflies and the plants. They learn what is good for the plants and what one should rather not do. In short, a child's flower bed becomes a microcosm and a place of experiment.

In time, young gardeners will also come to know the larger rhythms of the sun and the moon, the seasons, of birth and death. And finally they will learn that they themselves are part of this big cycle. This insight will teach them to be kind and careful in their treatment of nature, a first step towards the realisation that we are all mutually dependent and require an environment that is as healthy as possible.

In the abstract, this may all sound a bit unrealistic. Of course, the development of a child's relationship to nature generally does not take place consciously. It is rather the subliminal acceptance of a basic attitude towards the world around us. Children who interact with nature, even that small part of it contained in a garden, can learn responsibility and connectedness to the natural world. This can be more difficult for children who grow up far from nature.

The importance of a garden in giving children an opportunity to become familiar with nature and gain some basic practical knowledge of biology cannot be overestimated. To make the most of this opportunity, it is important for young gardeners to learn gradually to do all the jobs on their own, from sowing, planting, weeding and fertilising to watering, pruning and protecting plants (from frost and pests).

Particularly with very young children, it is a good idea to provide some playing space on the patio. The nearness of the play area makes it easier to watch over them.

WINDING PATHS

You can make a small garden seem larger by going into the third dimension. Give it vertical contour with raised beds, or allow climbing plants to range up the house or a pergola. The garden will also seem bigger if you put in angled or curving paths that are given added structure by hedges, conifers or shrubs.

Winding paths are a very attractive feature in a garden. And it is even better when they are slightly overgrown. Especially in a small garden, these two

your garden is and for what purpose the paths will be used. For a small track to an herb garden, 30 cm (12 in) in width is enough, while the main path, where two people may

A path winding its way to your house, climbing plants on the walls and plants arranged according to height not only make your garden seem larger, but add immeasurable charm.

aspects give paths a magic all their own, because curves and hedges can hide surprises, and plants between stepping stones or pavers help create a natural appearance. If you have a need for some sort of surfaced path, it will become apparent after every rainstorm. But the trick is in how you construct the "traffic network" in your small garden. The terrain is the determining factor. While you can build straight paths on a flat piece of land, on a slope it is better to put in a few curves. The size of the paths is also determined by how big

want to walk abreast or wheelbarrows will be used, may be up to 1.5 metres (5 ft) wide.

If you decide to use pavers, you should not place them too close together, but leave room for some green in between, if only grass. There is no harm in leaving half a metre (20 in) between the middle of one paver and the next, because then even ground cover plants will have a chance to grow. They soften the edges of the pavers or natural stone and even overgrow them in places, giving you a path that is solid, but not hard in appearance.

If a path leads across a lawn, placing the paving stones or groups of bricks slightly apart will allow you to mow around them more easily. The pattern they form and their colour also make a pretty contrast with the surrounding grass. This is one reason why it is good to put a few curves in the path and make it longer. But curves also serve to soften the effect of a path, especially when overhanging plants on the edges help conceal it.

On the other hand, you shouldn't exaggerate. Paths are a very useful structural element in a garden, so you want to strike a good balance with the surrounding plant growth. Good visual balance is particularly easy to see with gravel paths. Their light colour forms a stark contrast with their garden surroundings, so they can tolerate plants spilling over onto them in places. However, they should still retain some prominence. An edging or border of some kind serves another useful purpose

with gravel paths—it helps keep the gravel where you want it, preventing loose stones from rolling onto the lawn or into flower beds. Gravel has one very valuable advantage in winter, which is that it is unlikely to become slippery.

This combination of wooden planks, stones and ornaments makes a relaxed, natural impression.

A multi-level rose garden—wooden trellises, which are available in all heights, give support.

WATER FEATURES

Water features give any garden added freshness and vitality. No garden is too small; in fact, if there is very little room, you might even consider having just a water garden. Of course, this is only advisable if your garden exists purely for decorative purposes.

Water not only makes every garden a feast for the eyes, it also makes the space more vital and alive. Whether you decide on a stone trough, a garden pond or some kind of fountain is a matter of personal preference. No matter what you choose, the presence of water will give you numerous options when it comes to plants.

Normally, a pond, well or, very occasionally, a stream will only be one element in your garden and designed so as to harmonise with flower beds and lawns, hedges and plants. But it will still have a special status. Water is always fascinating because it is so changeable and has such an effect on mood. It reflects the blue sky in summer, is rippled by the wind and creates little splashes when heavy raindrops fall into it. A pond, well or large stone trough with water under a pump or tap makes the most powerful impression when it is situated in a sunny location. Plants that grow near or in the water will also thrive particularly well there. Small bodies of water are often surrounded by small shrubs, so leaves will not be such a great problem and you won't always have to be fishing them out.

Before you can enjoy your water feature, you will have to put a great deal of effort into constructing it. However, modern materials have made things much easier than they once were. A concrete pond, for which you would have to get in a company to do the work, will likely be more elaborate than required. For small gardens, it is advisable to put in pre-formed ponds, which you can find at a garden centre in many shapes and sizes. Putting in a pond using a plastic liner is more work, as you will have to dig a hole of the desired size and depth. For a variety of reasons, it is advisable to cut ledges down the sides of the hole. Various water plants like to grow at different depths, a gradual transition looks more attractive, and it is safer in case a child slips into the pond. You can make your pond more durable by using strong pond liner. With larger ponds, you will have to put down several layers and weld them together. You can obtain everything you need from the same company that sells the liner. Make sure you do not put in a pond like this near trees or shrubs, or the roots could bore holes in the plastic.

There is a wide range of plants for growing both in ponds and around them. It makes a charming effect to have some parts of the bank covered with stepping-stones or pavers and others with reeds or sand. Animals will come to settle in and near your pond of their own accord: dragonflies soon arrive, bees buzz around the flowering plants and birds come to drink.

In the water, tiny insect larvae will soon be followed by their predators, which are much more interesting to watch: the large water beetles, salamanders and frogs. You will have to put in fish yourself; they are the best destroyers of mosquito larvae. However, to keep fish, you will need a pond that is at least 80–100 cm (30–36 in) deep so that they can survive the winter in it.

This composition, with its mosaic wall, was quite a lot of work to create, but creates a soothing and artistic atmosphere (above).

SHAPED SHRUBS AND TOPIARIES

The variety of forms that nature produces entices us to produce some manmade, artistic variations in imitation. There are a large number of evergreen and deciduous plants that can be pruned into imaginative figures. These will attract a great deal of attention, both on their own and in contrast with their natural surroundings.

If you want to give your otherwise natural looking garden an artistic touch, you can create a huge range of shapes with your pruning shears: rounded, angular, symmetrical and asymmetrical figures will soon decorate your garden. Do keep in mind that it takes a lot of work.

You can quickly learn the methods needed for such surprising effects. You should start off with mesh sculptures that you fill with compost and cover with ground covering plants. There are no limits to the shapes you can create, because you are not manipulating the plants but creating the form yourself. That is why sculptures like these are only preliminary exercises for the green art works that you produce with the pruning shears.

First of all, you have to know what effects each cut has. If you clip off tips, you stimulate the plant to spread out and become fuller and bushier. By cutting off lateral branches you push the growth towards the top and make the shrub grow upwards. If you want to encourage a bud on a bare stem to shoot, making a notch above it will give it the impetus it needs.

You will produce the best results with box, which is very robust and can be shaped into almost any form. But it does grow very slowly. This has one advantage, however: you can make constant corrections and maintain the result for a long time with only a few snips every so often. Many gardeners use the easy shapeability of box to create rounded or curved figures—you can even create animal sculptures.

Hedges, whether they are the border for a block of land or structural elements in a garden, are the main field of activity for pruning. Many plants that grow well as hedges can be shaped to some degree, from privet and yew to hornbeam. For the most part, it is a matter of increasing density; cutting off the tips of branches from an early stage can encourage this. When the plant is only 30 cm (12 in) high, it is cut back

relatively easy to produce, while more complicated works of art require more patience. In difficult cases, even experts have recourse to temporary or permanent aids made of wire: a piece of mesh in the desired form is first placed over the plant as a guide for the shoots. Later, everything that overgrows this frame can be trimmed. Once the necessary thickness and shape have been achieved, the mesh is no longer needed, as then you can return to pruning free hand.

by half in mid-summer (in the case of deciduous shrubs, in autumn). You can allow low-growing conifers to grow to their full height and then prune them into the desired form.

During the later growth phase, the side shoots also have to be lightly pruned on a regular basis to give the shrub the required fullness. A good rule of thumb is to cut them back by one third. The first substantial shaping takes place after the shrub has been cut back four to five times. Cones and other simple shapes are

Classic garden symmetry—twin globes proudly guard the garden and the house (above left and above).

This bench is twice as cosy enclosed by small hedges (left).

99

SMALL TREES FOR SMALL GARDENS

Even if you have enough room for trees, many of the larger ones won't be suitable because they produce too much shade. But almost all trees exist in smaller forms, and some just naturally never get very large, so there is nothing to stop you having pretty autumn foliage and attractive blossoms (if you choose a flowering tree) in your garden.

> No garden is so small that it has to be without a tree. Even the false acacia (above) is available in a small variety that only grows to be 2 to 3 metres (7 to 10 feet) tall.

Almost everyone would like to have at least one tree in his or her garden. They certainly add character, in part because of the shade they provide. But that is also why you have to choose their location carefully. You don't want shade to become a problem rather than a boon. Many plants do not like to grow in shade. In addition, when planted near a house a tree can sometimes make the rooms it shades rather dark. Once it is planted and has attained a certain size, a tree is almost impossible to move and becomes a permanent fixture.

In order to avoid any unpleasant surprises, when buying a tree you should find out exactly how high it can be expected to grow. You should also tell whoever is advising you where the tree is to stand and what soil and light conditions it can expect in your garden. Only very robust trees are suitable for the north side of a house, which is generally draughty and rather sunless, while for the more sheltered southern side even a delicate peach tree might come into question.

In the chapter on fruit trees and shrubs, you will see that a number of extremely compact varieties have been developed. They should find a place in every ornamental garden, as they

blossom beautifully in spring, look splendid in late summer when laden with fruit, have colourful foliage in autumn, and stand out before the bright sky like silhouettes in winter.

Magnolias, on the other hand, are a purely decorative tree, if only for a short time in spring. They can spread their branches quite wide, so you should look for small varieties when buying one. If you put in a staghorn sumac nearby, you will be able to enjoy this corner of the garden once again in autumn, as the colour of its pinnate foliage is not to be beaten. One special tip: the bristly locust, only 2–3 metres (7–10 ft) tall, blossoms in May and then again in September.

Trees are so durable that would be easy to assume they do not need any care. This is a mistake, however. Of course, you will take all the necessary measures when planting a tree, but if you don't continue to look after it, it may well wither away. It needs care particularly when young: a tree is especially at risk from weather and pests while it is growing.

Wind is the number one danger for young trees. You should provide them with a support when they are first planted (by driving stakes into the planting hole) as the roots are still loose and cannot withstand any substantial amount of force. You can protect the stem best from rodent damage by wrapping a spiral of plastic sheeting around it.

In small gardens, trees are particularly good for edging lawns or creating a border to the property next-door (left).

Cherry trees blossom early, giving great pleasure with their abundant white (below) or—in the case of the Japanese ornamental cherry tree (opposite page, below)—pink flowers.

ROSES

In many cultures and since time immemorial, the rose has reigned as the queen of flowers, or even the entire garden. It has inspired poets and artists, but also breeders, who have cultivated an inexhaustible range of varieties. There is an ideal rose for every purpose and many locations, each with a beguiling fragrance and seductive beauty.

The rose is not only one of the best-known flowers, but also one of the most versatile. An archway of roses provides a romantic welcome. Roses are found as ground cover, as shrubs and as climbers. There are a breathtaking variety of types, species and cultivars.

Roses are by nature multi-talented. They come as shrubs, as climbers for trellises, as ground cover, as tree roses, as hedge roses, as wild looking briar roses or, trained to form a living fence. Whatever role you intend it for, you will find a rose that fits the job perfectly. The range and variety is so large that no comprehensive overview can be attempted here. And there is no point in singing the praises of the rose's incomparable beauty: writers more competent in the lyrical vein have already done that to perfection.

But there is a less familiar side to this plant, one that has only a limited amount to do with its aesthetic charms: its smell is sensuously intoxicating. A volatile oil was already being extracted from the petals of the rose in ancient times. It fills the air with a fine fragrance that even modern chemists cannot surpass. Rose oil was one of the first perfumes and is still an essential ingredient in perfume production.

The ancients reasoned that anything that smells this fabulous has to be good for you, or possibly even have curative properties. Cooks and apothecaries began to take an interest in the plant early on. Chefs made rose punch, served candied rose petals and developed rose jams. Winemakers used red rose petals not only to give white wine an attractive and appealing colour, but also to improve its taste and the mood of those who drank it.

Perhaps it was the effect of rose wine that made people look at other parts of the plants as well. The wood proved highly suitable for inlay work and small carvings. The hairy, nut-like hips could be made into a jelly that had healthful effects; we know today that this is owing to its high vitamin C content. The hips, which are sometimes taken as an infusion by people with kidney complaints, also contain malic acid, sugar and mucilaginous substances.

The climbing rose 'Paul's Scarlet Climber' (left) has lofty ambitions; the dog rose, Rosa canina, *is prettier than its name might suggest (right).*

The rose 'Fair Play' is here trained as a standard so that its blossoms hover elegantly above the ground (left); the rose shrub 'Eden' does credit to its name.

The short culinary and medical excursion above is meant to show why the rose was so highly esteemed throughout history. Its popularity today stems almost solely from its visual qualities and its ability to adapt to many different types of soil. However, it always needs soil that is permeable, rich in nutrients and well drained. The climbing roses also have a lasting claim on gardeners' affec-

of every imaginable hue. The forms of the flowers can also be very expressive. Single or double—you need the right instinct to make a choice.

There are around 250 species of rose growing in the wild. Some of these are cultivated as garden plants. They are eminently suitable for creating natural-looking

The floribunda rose 'Australian Gold' (above) makes one long for a glass of champagne; others have a seductive fragrance or create a romantic mood. Leafing through a catalogue or shopping for roses is often enough to turn people into devotees.

tion because of the way they can be used to decorate pergolas, walls and summerhouses. And there is one other aspect of their enigmatic magic that still remains relevant today: even modern lovers let roses do the talking when words fail them.

There is probably no other type of plant that produces such a range of different colours as the rose. They don't always have to be dark red. Pale pink can be a gentle hint, yellow an expression of pure joy, white a way of elegantly making contact—you can obtain roses

gardens. They barely need pruning and mostly only bloom once a year. The pretty fruits they bear make them attractive in autumn and winter as well. You can see what breeders have been able to do with some of them by the number of cultivars they have developed: in the nineteenth century, over a thousand variations of French roses alone.

One of the oldest cultivated forms is probably the Damask rose, whose name betrays its Syrian origins. They arrived in the west a thousand years before Christ and have sur-

Anyone wanting a sea of roses like this one (left) should make sure there is enough variety. Here, 'Fritz Nobis' and sweet briar have been combined.

vived here in numerous forms. For example, there are summer Damasks, which grow up to 2 metres (7 feet) tall, and the slightly smaller autumn version. From these are descended the Portland roses, named after the second Duchess of Portland, which in turn gave rise to the Noisette roses, developed in America.

One milestone was the tea rose, finally developed in 1830 after a long period of cultivation. It is very sensitive to cold and thus only to be recommended to experts. Crossing the tea rose with other rose groups produced hybrids with the tea rose's typical fragrance, intensive red colouring and long blooming period. There are around 8,000 varieties to be found in specialist catalogues, and new varieties are always being added. However, most of them enjoy only short success on the market before disappearing once more.

Among the bedding roses are the floribunda varieties, which include sub-groups with very large flowers. Miniature or dwarf roses are also suitable for small gardens. They are good for borders and small hedges; particularly small sorts can be used for ground cover. Standard roses (also called tree roses), which are grafted onto stems up to 1 metre (3 ft) high, are more suitable for small avenues or on their own. They also look good in containers,

making them a mobile form of decoration. So-called weeping roses are also standard roses, but here, climbing roses are used as grafts.

The white Damask rose 'Mme Hardy' (below) is an oriental beauty from Syria.

LAWN OR MEADOW?

However beautiful flower beds, shrubs, trees and hedges make your garden look, they only look half as attractive if they are not contrasted with areas more restful to the eye. It is a matter of taste and practicality whether these restful, uncluttered spaces consist of lawn or a flowery meadow. Sometimes both options can be included.

One of the more difficult decisions in a small garden: rather a green carpet that is ideal for children to play on—and for your deck chairs at the weekend—but needs care? Or a colourful, flowery meadow, more carefree once established, but purely for visual enjoyment?

A lawn can be relaxing both for the eye and in a more literal sense. It doesn't compete with flowers and blossoms, but provides a contrast. Moreover, a well-maintained lawn is usually so hardwearing that playing on it does no harm at all. A meadow, on the other hand, would be badly damaged. Even deck chairs or just walking on it will hurt it. A meadow is there chiefly for decorative purposes and is meant to be looked at, not played upon.

Or, at least, not by people—insects will indeed play upon it. This is another advantage of a flowery meadow. It attracts butterflies, bees and bumblebees, which your fruit and vegetable plants will also be glad to see. Beetles find a home in a meadow, along with many other small creatures. This makes a meadow more alive than a lawn, although the latter is more useful to people. The decision on what to plant is thus governed by both aesthetic and functional factors. If the size of your garden allows it, however, you can have both.

Let us first look at lawns as a horizontal structural element. If you put in one or more lawns among your other planting schemes, you can achieve amazing visual effects, for example, by edging them with beds. This gives your garden an impression of more depth than actually exists. If lawns are situated in curves between the various beds, they create a relaxed effect, while a square or oval lawn, used as a play area, becomes the heart of your ornamental garden.

Lawns, of course, need more maintenance than meadows, which only require mowing once or at most twice a year. Lawns have to be cut at least every fortnight for about half the year. If they are to look at all neat, they also need to be cultivated in spring and weeded in the warmer half of the year. Looking after the borders also takes some work. And lawns that are used a lot have to be repaired occasionally.

If you want a patch of meadow as well as a lawn, there is also a risk that flowers and plants from your meadow will spread to flower beds and lawn, making more weeding work in the entire garden. Meadow fans should therefore make sure that they mow the meadow before seeds are developed in summer. This will not work with all plants, however, so if

you want to put in a meadow, you should talk about it with your neighbours first. You can't expect them all to share your joy in the colourful flowers it produces.

Lawns and meadows can complement one another very nicely if you are not too meticulous. A closely mown, winding lawn path through your flowery meadow, around trees, or in front of benches creates a pretty colour contrast.

A patch of lawn and a few shrubs are enough to create a shady idyll (above).

BEDS FOR EVERY SEASON

Your garden need not look pale at any time of year. Blossoms or fruit provide colour in almost every month, although the time from March to October is the best in this regard. In winter there are always the evergreens, and it is not as hard to do without colour when one can hope for a sugar-like dusting of snow.

> At the outset everything must be planted, that's clear. But your efforts are not in vain: if you plan cleverly, you'll be rewarded with a garden bursting with blossoms the entire year through.

Colours begin to appear even before spring, and are especially bright and welcome after the grey months. Snowdrops provide a little green at first and herald the crocuses, for example, which soon steal the show from them in March at the latest. Even the greatest lawn fans do not mind a few amidst a green carpet, for no one can be angry at these small but cheerful bulb flowers with their amazing intensity of colour. And after they have ceased flowering, their leaves and stems do not disturb even in the most perfect lawn; they blend right in, almost in-

visibly marking the spot where these colourful blooms will announce the coming of spring again the next year.

Then come the larger, somewhat more spectacular bulbs already mentioned in the section on rock gardens: tulips take over from the crocuses. But they do not reign supreme for long, for narcissuses and forget-me-nots, hyacinths, daisies and bird-in-a-bush also want to play their part in the concert of colours. And the smaller flowers do not hide themselves, making up in numbers for that which they lack in size. Marguerites, as these small, white spring daisies are also called, are prettily sprinkled all over the lawn until it is cut for the first time. These little stars are also called bruise-wort. These days there are cultivars available in many colours and with large flowers that can even hold their ground in narcissus beds.

Bird-in-a-bush does not grow much larger. It displays its fine qualities in a venue much neglected by other flowers: shade. Bird-in-a-bush comes from the woods, where it has learnt to make the most of little light. These delicate little plants with their multi-lobe leaves produce clusters of bizarrely shaped, spurred, purple-violet flowers before the foliage of the trees blots out their sun. A number of garden varieties of bird-in-a-bush are available to give your spring flower beds a darker background colour.

For example, the radiant yellow flowers of the lesser celandine stands out well against these purple beauties. Lesser celandine is also a

A riot of colour: tulips, forget-me-nots, daisies and more in a beautiful spring mix (above).

Snowdrops ring in the flowering seasoning, but crocuses soon join them in the first colour play of the year (opposite page).

Daffodils, bird-in-a-bush and lesser celandine (left) harmonise perfectly in yellow and violet.

plant a weed. As long as you keep it under control by cutting it back and weeding it out thoroughly after it has bloomed, this little flower can be a valuable addition to the palette of your spring garden from March to May.

In May the first harbingers of summer begin to appear, for example, common mullein, also called candlewick plant or woollen. Oddly enough, this splendid perennial flower is not often found in our gardens. This could be because many gardeners find it overpowering, since it does grow to a height of up to 2 metres (7 feet). But this very boldness is what makes it interesting for small gardens, as it stands up tall and slender like a sunny exclamation point. Its strong stem usually needs no support. What's more, it is very tolerant with regard to soil and care, and looks attractive even after it has finished blooming because of its felted, yellowy green leaves.

Somewhat later, the cosmos flower puts in an appearance. This graceful annual bears large flowers with airy foliage. Colours range from white to blood red or nearly black, with every imaginable shade in between available (with the exception of blue). Although cosmos originated in high altitude, sub-tropical regions of America, it thrives in the U.K; it can withstand fairly inclement weather. However, it cannot tolerate frost and dies off as soon as the temperature

Summer is the time of floral abundance. It is difficult to choose, but almost every combination is perfect: bell flowers, mullein and cosmos (above); sweet alyssum, marigolds, marguerites and woodland sage (below); lady's mantle and day lilies (opposite side above) or box, yellow coneflowers, foxtails and geraniums (opposite page below).

woodland flower, and grows well in the shade of high daffodils, for instance. But be careful: lesser celandine tends to spread rapidly and many gardeners justifiably consider the small

drops below the freezing point. It is thus grateful for sun, but needs no fertilisation.

Now the chrysanthemums and later blooming daisies come into their own. They mix well with many plants, notably marigolds and woodland sage. Chrysanthemums are documented in early Chinese records, so they have been cultivated for a very long time. Even today there is a veritable chrysanthemum cult in Japan, which centres mostly on the six-rayed kind of this flower. In Europe the oxeye daisy is so wide-spread that many consider it to be a weed. Its flowers, which last into September, are white stars with yellow centres. There are very lovely cultivars of the closely related Shasta daisy, like the double 'Wirral Supreme' and the very free blooming 'Snowcap'. And what else begins to bloom in the marvellous abundance of early summer? Lady's mantle and day lilies and foxtails and geraniums (pelargoniums)—the choice is unending.

Amidst the myriad choices available, we will single out just one other summer flower that is not seen as often as it should be: the yellow coneflower, a long-blooming plant that comes

for your autumn garden. It has a large number of small flower heads with white petals, while the solid aster has no such petals, just radiant yellow disc florets. There are also a number of dwarf asters that form wonderful cushions of blue to pink late in the year.

Among the most popular flowers of late summer and autumn are the dahlias, which no garden—or, in the case of low-growing varieties, no balcony box—can afford to be without. They originated in America and although the first specimens were not brought to Europe until the early nineteenth century, they have had a meteoric career owing to the many cultivars. There are dahlias with disc flowers, made up of tube-

There's no need for autumn melancholy, as perennial sunflowers, Rudbeckias and grasses sweeten the shortening days (above).

As if they mean to outdo their summer relatives, dahlias and autumn asters bloom in all imaginable colours (right).

as an annual, a biennial and a perennial. It flowers up into autumn, when many of its garden companions have lost their lustre. Yellow coneflower gets its name from its large flower heads, which boast butter-yellow daisy-like petals and a dark brown central cone of tubular florets, which sometimes almost looks black.

The yellow coneflower, also known as Rudbeckia (after a clan of Swedish botanists), marks the transition to late summer and autumn. Pansies and perennial sunflowers are still in bloom, but asters and dahlias now take over and are presented in detail here:

Some asters bloom in the spring, but the autumn varieties are more popular. These include the Italian aster, which is also called Italian starwort because of the shape of its flowers. Garden centres carry a large number of cultivars that, like 'Lady Hindlip,' for example, are characterised by light violet-coloured petals and a heart of yellow disc-like florets. The variety 'King George' is a little darker. These perennials grow around 60 cm (24 in) tall. They like sunny locations and dry, porous, chalky soil.

The bushy asters, which come from America, grow to between 25 and 100 cm (10–36 in) tall. They retain their bright pink flowers until the first frost. The heather aster, densely branched and with fine foliage, provides lovely decoration

shaped florets, like the popular round, ball variety; and others with ray flowers, whose petals are flatter, like the outer petals of daisies or asters. These are further divided into single, semi-double, or double varieties. The most frequently encountered dahlias are those with blooms like bright yellow balls hovering on their stalks.

The variety of forms is even more confusing: there are single-flowered, anemone flowered, collarette, waterlily, decorative, ball, pompon, cactus and semi-cactus, plus a whole category devoted to miscellaneuous kinds that don't fit in. Without an advisor, you will be spoilt for choice. But there are some general rules for their care: they need rich, well-cultivated soil and

sun, shelter from wind; leave 50 cm (20 in) or more between plants, plant tubers 5 cm (2 in) deep in May, and water and feed generously in summer.

Certainly one of the best-known flowers, the pansy blooms very early in March or else quite late in the year.

PLANTS FOR SMALL GARDENS

HERBS

Herbs are among the oldest cultivated plants. Their ability to enhance food, alleviate or even cure various ailments and produce alluring fragrances was recognized very early on in history. Perhaps advances in modern medicine led to their being pushed out of the limelight. But now they are back in fashion, and rightly so. Small gardens in particular should not be without them.

No matter how small your garden, there is no doubt room for herbs, as they can grow between vegetables, under ornamental plants, in beds or in pots, on the balcony and by hedges. Many are ideal for edging beds, they can be planted in charming combinations between the spokes of an old wagon wheel, and they can beautify window

The variety of herbs and spices is almost immeasurably huge. By changing the mixtures and amounts, it is possible to create a never-ending array of new recipes and flavours. Rosemary is one of the most popular kitchen herbs. Its leaves and tips can be used both dried and fresh for cooking. It is also good for enhancing oil and vinegar.

ledges—and not just in the kitchen. Most of them need no more than sun and shelter from wind. If you use herbs frequently, you will want them growing near the house and easily accessible.

Although herbs look particularly attractive in company with other useful or ornamental plants, they can also be grown in an area set aside just for them if this seems more practical. When putting in an herb garden like this, which should be well enclosed, to keep in the inimitable fragrance and shelter them from the wind, you can imitate various models.

Medieval geometric patterns, like those used in the gardens of the famous abbess, theologian and herbalist Hildegard von Bingen, have a contemplative quality. In those days, the garden was a place of refuge and reflection, with wells to provide coolness, gravel paths for strolling upon, and summerhouses of jasmine or honeysuckle in which to while away the time. The smell of herbs stimulated both conversation and meditation, encouraging people to concentrate on the essential.

Sage (left) is not only a flavoursome herb, but has curative properties as well.

Like many other kitchen herbs, thyme (below) aids digestion, particularly after rich food.

If order and symmetry do not appeal as much as abundant cascades of these fragrant plants, one may put in a romantically overgrown terraced herb garden. This creates a natural effect and provides room for benches in a fragrant atmosphere, among tall-growing herbs such as elecampane, lovage or angelica. A farmyard style herb garden also makes for a natural impression with its combination of fruit trees and shrubs, flowers and herbs. Admittedly, you will need a certain amount of space for this, as fruit trees, even if they are not large, tend to spread.

As mentioned earlier, combination crops are important everywhere, including herb gardens.

Valerian (below) is not only one of the most popular herbal tranquillisers, it also effectively reduces high blood pressure and is sometimes recommended for heart problems.

Arranging your garden with plants of different types next to each other gives it more visual appeal and makes the plants more resistant. The pesticide exuded by the marigold, for example, protects potatoes from pests. Vegetables and fruit trees grow even better in the company of onions and garlic. And highly aromatic herbs like thyme, sage, savoury, rosemary, marjoram and hyssop attract bees and butterflies as pollinators.

One special tip for those who enjoy lawns: a lawn does not always have to consist of grass. There are also spreading herbs that do not mind being trodden on; on the contrary, only through contact do they really give off their pleasantly pungent aroma. Of course, they will only do for small areas. The chosen place should first be weeded carefully, then prepare the soil with coarse sand and compost. A splendid carpet of thyme will grow on such a carefully raked and trodden down patch of ground. Choose thymes with different coloured leaves, and your results will resemble a lush, green quilt. Chamomile is another plant that will grow as an aromatic lawn.

As mentioned earlier, modern medicine has made the curative properties of herbs redundant in many cases. But it has by no means managed to replace them completely. Many medicines, particularly homeopathic ones, are still manufactured using herbs as a basis. Aromatherapy also relies heavily on herbs. And of course, the main uses of herbs today take place in the kitchen. But don't forget to employ these versatile plants around the house more generally, where herbal bouquets, or floral bouquets containing herbs, can scent the air with a clean and very pleasing aroma. At any rate, herbs once again enjoy a high status. A few of the most common are described below:

Soups and vegetables are made tastier by the oniony taste of chives. The delicate flavour of lamb is heightened by rosemary. Mint gives sauces a poetic touch. Vinegar loses much of its rigour when sage is added, as sage is very good at moderating flavours. Pasta, game and

Another benefit of herbs is that they are a pleasure to work with in the garden: they are as a rule undemanding plants and require no special care. Some herbs, like dill, are annuals and have to be re-sown each year. More commonly, however, they are perennials that will grow year after year if they are given permeable soil and a sunny location. They tolerate dryness well, but occasional watering will be necessary during long rainless periods.

Many herbs are able to survive the winter outdoors if they are well-covered, although the more delicate kinds, such as basil, will do better inside. Many species have a tendency to spread, so it is a good idea to cut them back occasionally. This also revitalizes the plants, many of which sow themselves and can there-forebecome a nuisance. For this reason, you should deadhead herbs before they go to seed, unless you would like to have a supply of seeds for sowing.

fish can barely manage without marjoram. Tomatoes are only half as tasty without basil. Parsley gives many dishes a tangy, refreshing touch. Sour fruits can be made palatable with sweet cicely. Thyme turns many a main dish into poetry. Tarragon prevents chicken from tasting bland, and caraway aids digestion.

Lavender (left) is a valuable herb for many complaints, including headache, digestive problems and nervous disorders.

To make herbal oil the flowers, leaves, or other parts of the plants containing essential oils are soaked in cold-pressed vegetable oil (below).

By varying the herbs you add to an oil you can make wonderful flavoured oils or massage oils (above).

Mugwort is used for medicinal purposes, and occasionally as a bitter flavouring. The herbage is collected and dried during the blooming period, while the roots are gathered in autumn.

For small gardens, the smaller, lower-growing herbs that have been mentioned so far are of course the most suitable. If you have a little more room, however, some of the taller and larger shrubs and perennials are to be recommended. There will probably not be enough room for fully-grown trees, but bushes and half-shrubs at the edge of an herb garden create a nice border and are the best background for their smaller fellows.

Laurel trees, which grow up to 4 m (13 ft) tall, and even the 2.5-m (8-ft) tall varieties of elder will probably only be suitable in a few cases. But almost every garden will have room for the curry plant, as it grows to a height of only 60 cm (24 in). However, it does need protection in winter. Lavender should be included for its nostalgic fragrance alone, even if it can grow up to 90 cm (36 in) tall; it should be cut back in spring, without cutting the old wood. Wormwood, a member of the mugwort family, which belongs to the resilient half-shrubs and perennials, provides plenty of fragrance. Its silvery leaves also help tone down pure green foliage. Fennel has both culinary and medicinal properties. It is an umbelliferous plant

that grows from 1 to 1.5 metres (3–5 ft) tall. Russian comfrey is used more for medicinal than culinary purposes. It is as robust as its place of origin suggests. It likes humusy, damp soil with some sun and grows 40 cm (15 in) tall. In natural medicine, it is used to treat wounds that are not healing properly. Russian comfrey is eaten as a vegetable, its oil is used for flavouring, and the leaves are used for infusions to treat coughs and flatulence.

THE CURATIVE PROPERTIES OF HERBS

Teas, infusions and decoctions are increasingly popular in the treatment of various health problems. Many doctors recognize their effectiveness, so some of the apparent contradictions between orthodox medicine and alternative therapies have been disproven. This table shows the curative properties of the most important herbs.

Botanical name	Plant	Parts used	Dosage, form	Curative effect
Achillea millefolium	Yarrow	Whole plant dried when it first comes into bloom	1 tbsp to 1 glass water, infusion	Kidney and liver problems, lack of appetite, congestion of the veins
Althaea officinalis	Marshmallow	Leaves before it flowers	1 tbsp to 1 glass water, infusion	Respiratory ailments, inflammations of the bladder and intestines
Artemisia absinthium	Wormwood	Dried flowers and leaves	1 tsp to 1 glass water	Digestive ailments, insomnia, stomach and gall bladder ailments, metabolic disorders
Artemisia vulgaris	Mugwort	Dried roots, pulverised	1 tbsp to 250 ml water, boiled	Nausea, colic, cramps, stomach complaints
Bellis perennis	Daisy	Blooming plant, fresh or dried	1½ tsp to 1 glass water, decoction	Skin problems, bronchial asthma, fever
Berberis vulgaris	Barberry	Dried root bark	½ to 1 tsp to 1 glass water decoction	Diseases of the liver and gall bladder, jaundice, gout, rheumatism
Calendula officinalis	Marigold	Dried flowers and leaves	1 tsp to 1 glass water, infusion	Glandular infections, rashes
Crataegus laevigata	Midland hawthorn	Dried flowers or autumn fruit	1 tbsp flowers or fruits	Circulation disorders, anxiety attacks palpitations
Foeniculum vulgare	Fennel	Seeds	1 tsp to 1 glass water, infusion	Digestion problems, constipation, flatulence
Humulus lupulus	Hops	Dried fruit cones	1 tsp scales to 1 glass water, infusion	Insomnia, digestive problems, loss of appetite
Inula helenium	Elecampane	Dried roots, at least two years old	15–30 g (ground) to 1 litre water, infusion	Whooping cough, bronchial catarrh, bronchial asthma
Juglans regia	Walnut	Leaves	2 tsp (crushed) to 1 glass water	Digestive problems, anaemia, stomach and intestinal disorders, skin diseases
Juniperus communis	Juniper	Dried ripe berries	1 tsp crushed berries to 1 glass water	Bladder ailments, weak stomach, dropsy, metabolic disorders
Lamium album	Dead nettle	Dried flowers	3 tbsp to 250 ml water	Bladder and kidney ailments, insomnia, stomach ache
Lavendula angustifolia	Lavender	Dried flowers and leaves	1½ tsp to 1 glass water, infusion	Weak nerves, migraine, dizzy spells
Levisticum officinale	Lovage	Dried roots	Crushed, 1 tsp to 1 glass water, infusion	Respitory problems, migraine, loss of appetite, feeling faint
Matricaria chamomilla	Chamomile	Dried flower heads	2 tsp to 1 glass water, infusion	Colic, pain, gastroenteritis, infections or inflammations
Melissa officinalis	Baim	Dried leaves	3–5 g to 1 glass water, infusion	Loss of appetite, heart problems, weak nerves, colds
Mentha piperita	Peppermint	Dried leaves	2 tsp to 1 glass water, infusion	Intestinal and liver disorders, nausea, cramps, migraine, insomnia
Menyanthes trifoliata	Bogbean	Dried leaves	½ tsp to 1 glass water, infusion	Fever, stomach problems, headaches
Ocimum basilicum	Basil	Dried herbage and seeds	1 tsp to 1 glass water, infusion	Constipation, stomach cramps, bladder infections
Pulmonaria officinalis	Common lungwort	Dried leaves	2 tsp to 1 glass water, infusion	Laryngitis, tracheitis, bronchitis, influenza
Rosmarinus officinalis	Rosemary	Dried flowers and leaves	1 tsp to 1 glass water, infusions	Congestion, headache, circulatory disturbances
Ruta graveolens	Rue	Herbage dried while in bloom	1 tsp to 1 glass water, infusion	Breathing difficulties, palpitations, colds
Salvia officinalis	Sage	Leaves and young shoots	1 tsp to 1 glass water, infusion	Colds, breathing difficulties, inflammations of the liver and gall bladder, stomach ailments nocturnal sweats
Taraxum officinale	Dandelion	Leaves and roots, dried before the plant blooms	1 tsp to 1 glass water, infusion or decoction	Liver and gall bladder ailments
Thymus vulgaris	Thyme	Blooming herbage	1½ tsp to 1 glass water, infusion	Whooping cough, bronchial ailments stomach disorders
Tussilago farfara	Colt's foot	Dried flower heads and leaves, without stem	2 tsp to 1 glass water, boil briefly	Colds, loss of appetite, insomnia
Urtica dioica	Stinging nettle	Young leaves and roots, dried	1 tbsp to 250 ml water, infusion	Dropsy, liver ailments, gout
Valeriana officinalis	Common valerian	Dried rootstock	1 tsp (ground) to 1 glass water, as cold or hot infusion	Insomnia, nervous stomach and bowel disorders, migraine
Verbascum thapsus	Mullein	Dried flowers without calyxes	1 tsp to 1 glass water, infusion	Bronchial catarrh, cough, hoarseness, head cold
Verbena officinalis	Vervain	Whole plant including roots	1½ tsp to 1 glass water, as cold infusion	Exhaustion, stomach ailments
Viscum album	Mistletoe	Dried leaves, crushed	1 tsp soaked in 1 glass of cold water overnight	High blood pressure, cramps hardening of the arteries

Infusion: The herbs are steeped in boiling water, as for tea **Decoction:** The herbs are boiled in water, left a long while to draw, then strained off. **Cold infusion:** The prescribed amount is steeped in cold water and strained off after 8, 12 or 24 hours; the liquid is drunk. **Caution:** Do not drink herbal teas that you are taking several times a day for medicinal purposes for more than four weeks. The information in this table was gathered with great care. However, neither the author nor the publisher can assume any legal responsibility for any harm that may be incurred by following the above sugestions. The advice given here is no substitute for medical examination and supervision by a professional doctor. Please consult your proctor before undertaking any course of self-medication.

FRUIT TREES

Can you grow fruit on a little piece of land? Most definitely. Even if you have no more than a patio, you don't have to go without homegrown fruit, and the average garden is certainly big enough. There are now many kinds of apples and pears available in either dwarf or semi-dwarf varieties.

Winter pruning is an important aspect of maintaining apple and pear trees. It gives shape to the crown or the espaliered branches and encourages strong growth.

trees trained along wires or fences look just as decorative.

In order to do this, just plant a fruit tree near a supporting wall or structure and bend it in the desired direction, where it will find support and grow almost horizontally with its branches fanning out left and right. Fruit trees of every kind can also be grown in tubs. Tree nurseries offer special cultivars for this purpose, as the size of the tree is determined by the rootstock on which it is grafted. When buying a fruit tree, tell the person advising you where you intend to plant it. If it is destined for a container, you should purchase a tree grafted onto limited-growth rootstock.

A container "orchard" has the distinct advantage that it can be relocated in the cold season to your conservatory or greenhouse for added protection. This will even allow you to grow citrus or tropical fruit, if you have a relatively sunny patio or front garden. These plants would otherwise not survive the winter. The frost-tender peach with its characteristic narrow foliage and decorative fruit will also thank you for looking after it in this way.

One possibility for growing fruit where space is at a premium is to eliminate the trees' need to form a large, supporting trunk. Espaliered fruit that has been trained to grow along walls not only carries as good a crop as any free-standing tree, it also looks beautiful—whether in full bloom, with plump, colourful fruit on the boughs, or as a graphic bare-branch sculpture in winter. Fruit

Stone and pip fruits can also be trained on a trellis (left).

Pears (below) not only taste extremely good as fresh fruit, they are also ideal as cake toppings or stewed fruit.

Though espaliered fruit trees take up little space, they can still produce a good crop (above).

In late summer, even grapes grown along the side of your house can taste delicious, provided they have seen enough sun (right).

Fruit trees intended to grow in tubs are sold in large containers. Before you put the plant in the largest possible pot available, prepare the pot to ensure good drainage by covering the drainage holes in the bottom with stones or gravel. Then fill it with compost, or soil mixed with a lot of organic material, and press it down gently, layer by layer. Remove the plant from its container and place it in the prepared tub at the same depth it was in its original container and add soil to fill in around the sides. These plants need regular watering, especially if they have no access to rainwater, for example on patios. Add compost every two weeks during the growth period to increase the size of your crop.

Small container trees can bear a surprising amount of fruit, but if you have suitable walls or other support structure for espaliered fruit, you'll achieve a better crop of classic fruits like apples and pears from these larger plants. As many varieties are suitable for storing, you'll have a good source of vitamins from your own garden well into winter. Apple and pear trees—apart from espaliers, which need more pruning—are among the lowest-maintenance fruit trees of all. However, most will need a suitable pollinator in the vicinity (generally another fruit tree of a similar kind). Seek some advice on this to ensure you are not disappointed with the crop.

Whether you grow an espaliered or a free-standing tree, the planting and care routine is exactly the same. To nurture a healthy fruit tree, be it a pear or an apple, choose a plant in the autumn or winter with bare roots (if you're going to be growing it directly in garden soil) and plant it as soon as you get it home. To do this, dig a planting hole that is twice as wide as the root bale. Just to one side of the centre, ram a stake firmly into the ground, place the tree into the hole at the same depth as it was previously growing (you can easily tell by looking at the trunk) and fill the hole with good garden soil. Tread this down firmly against the roots, water the plant and apply a layer of mulch to the top layer of soil to help retain moisture. Tie the new tree to its stake with a piece of twine. If there is any danger of rabbits nibbling at it, protect the plant with a wire netting wrapped around the trunk.

Looking after the tree is simple. Mature apple and pear trees need pruning in winter. You do this to shape the crown or espaliered branches and encourage strong growth. Trees that bear fruit on the tips of their shoots will also need a revitalising cut. These branches need to be pruned back to the point where they join the relevant branch.

Whether apple or pear – a laden fruit tree is the epitome of late summer and autumn bounty.

> Berries fresh from the canes are better than almost any other fruit, yet they need relatively little maintenance once you have planted them.

BERRY FRUIT

Try and reserve a place in the sun for your berry canes if you want them to reward you with plenty of plump, ripe fruit. If trees or walls cast shade on the plants, the berries may sulk in the foliage, and neither currants nor strawberries like draughts or wind whistling through them. Otherwise berries are relatively low-maintenance plants.

In the previous section we saw that even large stone fruit varieties can find room in a small garden. Berry fruit is even better suited to small spaces, as the plants are naturally smaller and these days even come as balcony cultivars. There's no need to plant straggly canes any more if you want gooseberries or blackberries. Gardeners now tend to favour the smaller plants that bear fruit like miniature trees, making it easier to pick.

A desire for gardening convenience has given us wonderful new varieties. There are now

more at your disposal, you can choose a traditional bush. This fruit thrives on sunshine, but will tolerate a moderate amount of shade. Still, this simple rule holds true: the less sun, the smaller and sourer the berries. You can expect to harvest a bumper crop if you plant gooseberries in nutrient-rich, moist, humus-rich soil in a sunny position.

Water the plants continually while the fruit is ripening, as they are particularly thirsty at that stage. Well-rotted manure in the autumn and spring will also increase the crop. Mildew can be a major threat to gooseberries, so be sure to prune spent wood to rejuvenate the bush after picking the berries, leaving no more than a dozen two-year-old spurs cut back by one third. Remove any older wood and new shoots just above ground level. Mildew-resistant varieties of gooseberries are also available.

July and August is harvest time for most gooseberries (left).

They always taste best when you pick them yourself—plump and juicy raspberries.

blackberries with no thorns, compact versions of blueberries and cranberries, strawberries in hanging baskets or containers and even climbing strawberry plants on the market. These smaller-sized plants are equally suitable for borders, so you can help yourself to their fruit as you walk around the garden. The same is true for grapes, which will grow into juicy morsels along sunny, wind-protected walls.

But let's stay with the classic berry fruits and start with gooseberries. Select dwarf or espalier plants if you don't have much space. If you have a little

Gardeners who prefer sweeter fruit often plant raspberries. They are decorative throughout their long flowering period from May to August, have a delicate fragrance, and provide a daily supply of light red, juicy berries for many weeks in summer and early autumn. Raspberries are planted in rows, either in spring or in autumn, ideally with intervals of about 40 cm (15 in) between the plants. Leave only two rods on any new plants and trim them back to 20 cm (8 in), so that young shoots will develop and bear fruit the year after next.

Because the canes only last two years, the old wood must be removed after a time. The six young shoots left on the plant each autumn will then take on the task of supplying new berries. Cover the roots of the plants with a little mounded earth and a thick layer of grass clippings or compost (mulch) to stop the soil from drying out. Raspberries prefer moist, nutrient-rich soil conditioned with plenty of natural compost and will reward you richly with berries if you give them a sunny position. Tie the canes to wires, as they do grow very tall and can bend over or develop into ugly bushes that will become hard to pick.

The third of the classic berry fruits is the currant. There are redcurrants and less commonly white ones, which have a similar, sweet-sour flavour. The third kind,

Blackcurrants are a valuable source of vitamins. They produce fruit on last year's wood. If a young bush doesn't seem to have enough branches, cut all the shoots back radically in autumn.

blackcurrants, have a unique and slightly tangy flavour that is difficult to describe. They are popular ingredients for jams and exquisite jellies. It is not only the fruit that make currant bushes useful plants in every sense of the word, but also the fact that the bushes can form handy, fruit-bearing hedges.

An undemanding, winter-hardy plant, the currant bush will settle for virtually any soil available, but prefers a humus-rich, moist ground. Because the plants have very shallow roots, they tend to dry out quickly, so try to counteract this by watering them well and applying plenty of mulch around the base of the plants. They will not object to shady locations, but the crop will be bigger if the bush gets plenty of sun. Regular pruning to rejuvenate the plants will also contribute to an increased harvest. Don't leave anything older than three-year-old wood on the plant when you're pruning.

To conclude this discussion of berries, let's take a brief look at the blackberry. Very similar in shape to the raspberry, its dark blue-black fruit is more hidden by the foliage and has a more intense flavour. Ripe wild blackberries are especially delicious but not suitable as garden plants, as they are grow much more rampantly than the cultivated varieties and produce smaller and fewer fruit. Sun is the life-giving force of the blackberry bush, which is an otherwise quite undemanding plant. Just make sure that you prune the wood back vigorously in late winter, removing all but four to seven of the stronger new shoots.

PERENNIALS IN YOUR FLOWER GARDEN

This family of plants has already been introduced in the context of the rock garden, where you probably gained a sense of the great variety on offer. In this chapter additional perennials are presented, which still represent only a small fraction of all the available kinds. A few repetitions are inevitable, as some mentioned in the context of rock gardens simply can't be left out of any discussion of perennials.

In any herbaceous perennial garden there must be other plants to ensure the perennials are set off to advantage. These might include shrubs or perhaps a clump of reeds around a garden pond. Perennials look great in front of a lawn or as a colourful backdrop to green grass. Their beauty is also enhanced by smaller annuals that can be planted or sown between them. Evergreen ground covers make a very decorative border around perennial beds, tall grasses underline the opulence of the flowers, and dark conifers form an attractive contrast to their vibrant colours.

Other elements can also be combined with perennials. These hardy plants stand out well against wrought-iron fences or garden walls entwined with climbers. Right next to the house they add a feel-good factor, as their visual appeal is enhanced by their fragrance. This is why perennials are good choices for planting between paving stones on the patio or even in large tubs in an inner courtyard. Wherever you decide to grow them is really up to your own personal taste. Your own eye will tell you when you have applied the right dose of colour to each location.

Creating different visual layers is also important. It goes without saying that taller perennials should be planted at the back and other varieties graduated in size towards the front. This allows them all to flourish and make maximum impact. If you only have a very small section, it's worthwhile trying a circular flower bed of perennials in the centre of the garden. In this case, graduate the plants in size from the outside to the middle, to create a mound of flowers in the heart of the circle. It's important to create variety not only in the height of your perennials but also in the terrain of your garden. If you don't already have a garden on a hilly site, you can build mounds or banks to increase your planting area. You can also accentuate different levels by adding stepping stones, little stairs and certain perennials to make the hills seem higher, or ground-hugging dwarfs that make the little hollows appear deeper.

ANEMONE

Called bush wind or wind rose in some languages, after their Greek name (*anemos* means "the wind"), anemones are one

of the most popular perennials thanks to their prolific blooms. They come in many different colours and grace our gardens from spring until autumn. The blooms are particularly impressive because the plants themselves usually only grow about 24 cm (10 in) high, apart from a few taller cultivars.

Almost all anemones will survive through the winter, thanks to their underground storage organs (bulbs, roots or rhizomes). Some varieties grow wild as white or pink woodland flowers, although they tend to prefer the more southern regions of Europe. The 'Blue Shades' anemone, for instance, comes from the mountainous regions of Greece and Turkey.

The autumn flowering varieties of Asian origin are particularly popular in northern Europe. They arrived here about 150 years ago and by now have a firmly established place in many perennial gardens. This may have something to do with the fact that they tend to grow quite a bit taller than their European cousins. These perennials come in many colours and cultivated forms. They are usually sold as Japanese autumn anemones and flower from August onwards.

ASTILBE

A very pretty garden perennial that favours partial shade is the astilbe, with its distinctive feathery plumes. A member of the saxifrage family, this is a low-maintenance, moisture-loving plant. Despite its easy-care nature, it produces plenty of plume-like panicles of dainty looking flowers. We distinguish between the Chinese variety that only grows to be about 40 cm (15 in) high and comes in light or dark pink, and the Japanese astilbe that stands almost twice as high. One of this range, 'Brautschleier' (bridal veil) produces open sprays of pure white blooms in July, while the 'Superba' flowers a pink-purple and the 'Red Sentinel' a shimmering deep red. Some hybrids gracing cottage gardens from July to September grow up to 1 metre (3 ft) high or even taller.

SWEET WILLIAM

This member of the *Dianthus* genus is related to pinks and carnations, of which there are so many varieties and forms that even experts cannot keep track of all of them. Here sweet William will serve as our example:

Sweet William is often grown as a biennial, and also grows wild in many parts of Europe. It has established itself across many countries from the Pyrenees to China. It has single or compound blooms that range from white or pink to deep, dark red and all tones in between. A whole bed of these in different colours is a sight to behold in any cottage garden. Sweet Williams' dense flowers sit at the end of 25 to 70-cm (10–27 in) forked stems and the leaves are symmetrical, as in all carnations. The crown of the blooms is made up of five whiskery tufts that sit atop a narrow stem and have serrated petals. The whole plant may be tinged to a greater or lesser degree with bluish circles or "eyes". After flowering, it produces seed capsules that should be left to dry so the plant can self-seed.

BERGENIA

Evergreen, pink or red flowering bergenias (also called elephant's ears) are suitable for almost any soil in a moist, semi-shaded to sunny position. It is not just the blooms that appeal to flower gardeners, but also their large dark-green, shiny leaves that grow heart-shaped around the base and shoot up out of a thick clump of stems. This garden perennial, which only grows 30 to 40 cm (12–15 in) high, looks particularly good beneath larger shrubs. The original home of the bergenia is in the Himalayas and other mountainous regions of Kashmir. In these rugged environs bergenias acquired their hearty survival instincts, but also a tendency towards small blooms. Cultivars have since been developed and much larger flowering hybrids are now available. Some of them bloom in April or May and then produce a second crop of flowers in the summer. Other varieties display reddish brown foliage in autumn and winter. Propagation of these low-maintenance perennials is simply achieved by lifting and dividing the rhizomes with a sharp knife.

SPEEDWELL (VERONICA)

This is a perennial that meets many needs. Speedwell grows in dwarf form as a ground cover, happily plays second fiddle as a blue or purple companion to larger flowers or, in its American form, towers up 2 metres (7 ft) high. There are native varieties that many gardeners attack like weeds, while their counterparts from southern Europe or Asia are cultivated for their beautiful grape-like or candlestick flower formations, since the small blue varieties make up for their lack of size with the number and concentration of their blooms. Among the generally preferred, moderately tall varieties is the gentian-leafed speedwell, with its broad, pointed leaves on 30-cm (12-in) stems. The leaves form a rosette around the countless light-blue flowers that appear in May and June. The grey candle veronica forms dense clump-like bushes of a similar height. It gets its name from its silvery-grey, hairy foliage above which its dark blue flowers make a striking statement.

Other varieties grow twice as tall, such as the 'Schneeriesin' ("snow giant"), which seems a little out of character for these typically blue flowering plants with its snowy white blooms.

ACONITE

Originally a European woodland native, aconite or monk's hood is seldom found growing wild and is now a protected species in parts of Europe. It is still frequently found in the garden, as it produces prolific helmet-shaped, hanging blue goblet flowers that stand up like candles in clusters of bloom. This plant is not recommended for family gardens, as children tend to ignore warnings about the plant being poisonous. Monk's hood contains the neurotoxin aconitine that was once used to kill wolves. Quite a range of these herbaceous perennials is now available. Wolf's bane, for instance, whose name reflects the drastic measures once taken against the predator, is different from most cultivars, as it has light yellow flowers and grows 1.5 metres (5 ft) tall. Blue or bluish-white is a more common colour for this group of plants, and is a feature of the mountain aconite. Semi-shady or shaded positions and moist, cool, humusy soil are what this plant prefers. This is why wild monk's hood tends to grow at the edge of the woods and around bushy shrubs. If you only have a very sunny position to offer it the plant will grow, but it will need regular watering. This perennial will survive the winter quite happily.

FOXGLOVE

Another herbaceous perennial with potentially poisonous qualities is the foxglove, or digitalis. All parts of this plant are poisonous, but those very substances are the basis of an effective prescription medication for heart patients.

Foxglove is frequently found growing wild in European woodlands, sometimes in large groups, as the woods offer the right conditions for it to thrive: partial shade and moist, humus-rich soil that is low in lime.

The most widespread purple or red foxglove forms a 50-cm (18-in) high rosette in the first year, from which the flower stem emerges. It can reach grand heights of up to 1.5 metres (5 ft) and, as the Latin name suggests (*digitalis* = digit or finger), it is covered with blooms shaped like the fingers of a glove. This plant not only comes in red or blue but also yellow or white varieties.

The large-leaf foxglove or *Digitalis grandiflora* has particularly long foliage, which is slightly hairy on the upper side, and its creamy white or light yellow flowers can be well over 4 cm (1 in) long. Foxgloves are self-sowing plants.

GOLDENROD

Goldenrod is a popular garden perennial with a long tradition as an ornamental and healing plant. It flowers a vibrant yellow from July through to autumn. It is still used today in some herbal teas as a diuretic. Golden rod is an ideal border plant, with tall sprays of willowy flowers that seem to bring sunshine to the garden.

The plant itself needs a good amount of sun, partly to beautifully highlight its light yellow colour, but also to ensure that it is pampered at least from above, for as far as the soil is concerned, it will make do with almost anything.

One of the favourites among gardeners is Canadian golden rod. It is capable of displaying almost all the shades of autumn on its own. Many are hybrids that stretch more than 2 metres (7 ft) tall. Their thick stems are very hairy. The same variety comes in dwarf form and is particularly suitable for rock gardens and small plots. You will still have a dazzling show from this beautiful flowering plant as late as October. The giant golden rod surpasses all, by reaching heights of up to 3 metres (10 ft), while the European native or common golden rod is a much more humble variety. It does spread quickly though, and may take over if you let it. Cut back the stems immediately after flowering if you want to prevent this undesired effect.

BERGAMOT

This hardy, herbal plant is sometimes known in Europe as Indian nettle, referring to its North American origins, and its botanic name *Monarda* also tells a story. The first person to describe it was the Spanish doctor Nicolas de Monardes back in the sixteenth century. Bergamot develops single or multiple flower heads with arching, tubular, purple to red flowers growing from a circular centre, with reddish-coloured bracts. This has made the plant a popular ornamental, while the bergamot oil it produces also fascinates the essential oil and liqueur manufacturers.

Its aromatic fragrance means the plant always contributes to a pleasant atmosphere. It grows about 1 metre (3 ft) tall, has egg-shaped leaves that rest on pointy stems, and flowers from July through September. The bergamot will make do with any kind of soil conditions and prefers sunny to semi-shady positions.

However, you do need to watch that it doesn't become overgrown, as this New World plant can also be quite rampant.

MULLEIN

We have already met this lanky perennial in the chapter on early summer flower beds. The mullein is less common as a perennial than as a biennial, which is surprising, as the herbaceous perennial form is very easy to look after, undemanding and a metre-high (3-ft plus) flowering delight in glorious pale yellow every year.

There are many kinds available, but the dark mullein is worth a special mention. It grows from 60 to 90 cm (24–36 in) high, producing candelabra-like stems with attractive felted grey leaves. The long flower spikes feature densely packed yellow chalices with purple woolly filaments. Hybrid mulleins have been

cultivated with various growth habits, so there are now both towering and more compact varieties suitable for any size garden.

The mullein prefers a warm, sunny location with permeable soil, but otherwise has no special demands. It does, however, have a strong tendency toward hybridisation, so it is advisable to cut it back soon after flowering has ended.

Herbal tea drinkers may be interested to know that blooms stored in airtight containers can be brewed as a treatment for bronchial congestion. Oil pressed from the fresh flowers has also proved therapeutic for rheumatic conditions.

PASQUE FLOWER

This plant cropped up in the chapter on rock gardens, where there was less space for detailed information. Despite competition from plenty of other flow-

ers, the pasque flower has a special place among spring ornamentals, thanks to its large goblet-shaped flowers. Of the thirty or so naturally occurring

varieties, a few are native to Europe. They are closely related to the anemone, the yellow pheasant's eye or ranunculus family and the liverleaf, though

they are usually taller than their relatives. Dwarf varieties are nonetheless available for the smaller garden.

Some forms of the pasque flower were used in traditional medicine for such diverse complaints as menstrual problems, bronchitis, rheumatism and skin irritations. The latter is remarkable, given that even picking the flowers can often produce rashes. The substances given off by the tiny hairs on the blooms, leaves and stems can be a skin irritant. Pasque flowers need well-drained soil and should be left where they were originally planted. The older the plant, the less it will tolerate being transplanted. Their rootstocks will not recover once they have been disturbed.

LUPINS

In many cottage gardens you will find a classic duet of perennials: daisies teamed with perennial lupins. The two complement each other beautifully. Both thrive under the same conditions and produce their butterfly blooms and decorative foliage at the same time, in high summer.

Lupins are available in many different colours, from white, pink and yellow to purply-blue. There are even some two-toned kinds among the hybrids. They are shown to best advantage when grouped in different coloured bunches within the same flower bed, though tone-in-tone, such as red and pink, also go well together. If you remove the old flowers as soon as the the erect stems—which reach a good metre (3 ft) high—have finished blooming, you will stimulate new flower growth.

Lupins like a well-drained, slightly acid soil and partially shady to sunny locations. Their bright colours appear particularly intense in semi-shaded places.

In dry conditions, these pretty perennials will require regular watering, as the tall fully-grown spikes can become quite brittle. This is another reason it is advisable to allocate them to a bed that is well sheltered from the wind.

MEADOW SWEET

Meadow sweet is a member of the rose family, a perennial that is also known as queen of the meadows. Unlike the rose, however, it bears the tiniest of flowers atop 45-cm (18-in) stems, but they tend to cluster in dense panicles, which makes them capable of holding their own with many other head-turners. This is particularly true of the red varieties, while the white ones are slightly more restrained and demure. Some cultivars can reach heights of 1.5 metres (5 ft) and add lovely decorative flair to cottage gardens.

With the exception of the dropwort, or the bulb variety, all kinds of meadow sweet prefer moist to boggy ground in sunny or semi-shaded locations. This is no reason to relegate them solely to the direct vicinity of ponds or water features, but it does mean they will need regular watering if they are planted in a drier place.

Abundant clusters of meadow sweet are always eye-catching features, but individual plants are also attractive when flanked by ornamental grasses, purple loosestrife and bellflowers. Propagation is simply a matter of dividing the plant and letting it flourish anew.

PHLOX

Here is another familiar face from the rockery, about which a great deal more can be said, as the phlox family is a very extensive one. Moss phlox and other mound-forming varieties make good ground-hugging cushions of colour in any garden setting that is sunny or semi-shaded. They are content to live in average-quality soil as long as it drains well, but thrive best in a sandy, humus-rich ground.

Teamed with aubrietia, yellow alyssum or white alpine cress, the smaller phlox cultivars provide particularly effective splashes of colour in spring.

Medium height or taller phlox look good in between the lower cushion varieties with chrysanthemums, asters, early sunflowers and other yellow flowering plants. The taller varieties look very appealing surrounded by ornamental grasses. Phlox needs plenty of moisture and will therefore need extra watering on dry days. If you trim the stems by about a third immediately after the flowering period, laterals will be formed that later produce a second show. These perennials will not tolerate pressure from tree roots, so keep them some distance away from larger shrubs.

DELPHINIUMS

The delphinium is native to the temperate climes of northern Europe. New varieties of this congenial flower are continually being developed. There are mid-sized ones that stand 1 metre (3 ft) high, 2-metre (7-ft) tall giants and smaller versions that don't make it past the 40-cm (15-in) mark. Many delphiniums will flower twice a year if you cut them back by one or two hand-widths before seed forms. Most of the hybrids love sunny positions and loose, uncluttered soil. Because of their bright locations, these perennials need plenty of water, so it's a good idea to carve a little groove in the soil to catch water around the base of the plant.

Place delphiniums in front of a dark background like a wall or conifer so their lush, upright flower spikes can add height and drama to your garden. Cultivars come in many different shades that can be grouped together to produce a riot of colour. This can continue for five to eight years, in the case of the hardier perennials, after which they will need to be transplanted. Apart from regular additions of compost shortly before bud burst, and a stake for taller varieties, these dramatic plants need no special care or attention.

SALVIA (SAGE)

The Latin name of this plant—which occurs as a herb, a semi-shrub and a perennial plant—means "healing", and it has a long history as a medicinal plant dating back to antiquity. Sage came to Europe from the Mediterranean region back in the early Middle Ages and was cultivated in monastery gardens. It is still used in natural healing today and appears in products like throat lozenges. Of course, it has since gained real prominence as a kitchen herb.

The many different names of ornamental varieties of this plant reveal much about its versatility: Mediterranean sage grows to about 1 metre (3 ft) high and has yellowish-white blooms; meadow sage is purple-flowering; mealy sage has greyish-white, hairy stalks; the scarlet red woodland salvia or sticky sage; the common sage, with its wrinkly, felted leaves and pale purple flowers, only reaches 60 cm (24 in) tall; the pale blue clary sage; or the naturally popular 'Blaze of Fire' salvia, whose name says it all. This is definitely the virtuoso among them.

YARROW

Bring some gold into your garden by making room for a perennial that is undemanding, yet will reward you for even minimal care by producing striking, flat heads of yellow flowers. The rather prosaically named yarrow adds a touch of glamour to any summer garden. The flower heads rise up out of fernlike, dark green foliage, are lovely in combination with grasses or fiery red perennials and make a truly striking statement when set against a dark background.

The stalks grow more than a metre (3 ft) high and hardly have any leaves in their upper regions, which is why they look best against a lush backdrop. One particularly good variety for small gardens is the 'Coronation Gold' cultivar. It lives up to its royal name too, as its blooms are quite stunning, despite its smaller overall size. If you have more space in your garden, you can plant one of the standard varieties such as 'Gold Plate' or 'Cloth of Gold'.

Yarrow grows in all kinds of soil, even chalky ground, but it prefers nice and dry humus-rich soil and only needs occasional watering during extended dry spells. This robust perennial doesn't need wind protection but will require a little staking if it is planted in windy areas, so you may want to save yourself the bother by choosing a more sheltered spot.

HELEN'S FLOWER

The different varieties of the richly flowering, long-lasting perennial called Helen's flower grow between 50 cm and 1.5 metres (20 in–5 ft) tall. In the wild, this fine lady flowers in spring, but in a garden the cultivated forms take a little longer. They eventually appear in their yellow, brown or dark red finery and enjoy the company of other flowering perennials such as asters, delphiniums, daisies, or phlox. Helen's flower feels quite at home among tall ornamental grasses, because its rich finery stands out all the more.

Despite its frilly flower, this plant makes no extravagant demands on the gardener but will grow best in full sunlight. Helen also favours a nice humusy soil, as long as it isn't permanently damp. This perennial still needs plenty of watering though, to stop the foliage from turning yellow during any dry spells. Scatter some all-purpose manure around the plant three times a year, as it draws a great deal of nutrients from the soil. Should the flower display fade, the plant probably needs to be relocated.

Spring is the best time for transplanting and cutting back any spent flower stalks, but this graceful little lady needs no special winter protection.

CONEFLOWER

In the section about flower beds for all seasons, we touched on this decorative perennial. Now for some additional information: the coneflower (*Echinacea*) ranges in size from 30 cm to 2 metres (1–7 ft), so there is bound to be one for every purpose. There are yellow varieties of coneflower, but the kind most often seen are the purple or mauve sorts known as purple coneflower.

This colouring is highly attractive, providing a pleasing contrast between the petals and the dark brown or black "eye" at their centre. The dark green of the foliage makes the brightly coloured flowers all the more appealing. If sown early, you can enjoy a good show of blooms in the first year. The coneflower looks particularly striking in sunlight and it loves a sheltered, sunny position, although it will also grow in a semi-shaded spot. Soil should be moist but well drained. If there is any danger of it drying out in summer, add plenty of organic material to the soil. Though this perennial will survive the winter, a good layer of mulch will surely do no harm.

It's advisable to remove any deadheads if you don't want to collect the seeds. After four or five years you will need to divide the plant.

RED VALERIAN

The robust red valerian with its clusters of red (or, despite its name, white) flowers is a must for any self-respecting cottage garden. It grows about 50 cm (18 in) high and is an ideal border for any sunny site. It pays to keep these plants in check, though, as they are inclined to take over if left to their own devices.

The popular red version will add nice bands of colour to your herbaceous perennial garden between delphiniums or tall bellflowers. The same is true when you combine it with ornamental grasses. Dry places where other plants would not thrive make red valerian feel quite at home. However, this plant does need a rather chalky, low-nutrient, loose soil. Though it prefers warmth, it will survive the winter without special protection. To propagate red valerian, carefully remove the rootstock from the ground in the spring and divide it with a sharp knife.

MASTERWORT

The woodlands of Europe and West Asia are the home of the masterwort, which is why it thrives in our similar climate. It makes up for its small flowers by presenting them in pin cushion masses, set off by a ruff of large, green leaves which radiate from their stems.

The large masterwort (*Astrantia maxima*), which grows up to a metre (3 ft) high and has lobed, long-stemmed foliage, is the most common cultivar. It produces distinctive pink flowers from June to August and its

raised leaves are a little paler—sometimes even white.

The garden cultivar 'Rosea' has particularly beautiful flowers up to 4 cm (1.5 in) in size, and its lobed leaves are also much bigger than those of its wild cousin. The masterwort thrives in fresh, moist, nutrient-rich soil and will tolerate a sunny or semi-shady position. Otherwise it needs no special attention. When it comes to propagation, it is equally uncomplicated, unless of course you take exception to it self-seeding.

140

CRANESBILL (GERANIUM)

The cranesbill was introduced in the chapter about rock gardens. Here some additional information about this useful and beautiful plant:

There is a fitting cranesbill (hardy geranium) for almost every corner of the garden. There are sturdy types available that look good as ground cover under other perennials—like the 'Ballerina'. The more delicate forms look pretty in a tub with their tufts of light, soft, greenish-grey leaves and purple chalices, while a slightly larger cultivar called 'Lawrence Flatman' is also worth considering.

In some areas it is advisable to wait until spring before planting out plants with well-developed roots. By winter it will have formed sufficient rootstock to survive the colder months. This perennial is used to the sun from its mountainous homeland, though it also tolerates semi-shade. The soil should be permeable, yet conditioned with a little compost. The cranesbill will survive a frost, but is not keen on earth that is frozen solid. To prevent this you can add a little sand to the soil. This will also stop any water from gathering around the roots.

In the autumn, cut the plant back a bit to encourage good foliage growth. In the spring, remove any dead foliage from the young shoots.

DEAD NETTLE

A rather weed-like and well-established plant, dead nettle is often underestimated. Yet it flowers in various colours, and only grows up to 50 cm (18 in) high, so it is ideal for growing in large clusters that form mini pagoda shapes under shrubs. The gold variety also lights up the semi-shaded areas of the garden with its white-green variegated foliage. It will form a pleasant green carpet until well into winter.

Two other varieties are worthy of special mention. The spotted dead nettle forms a superb ground cover and flowers purple and pink from April until well into summer. It gets its name from its white spotted petals. The balm-leaved red dead nettle only comes as a garden cultivar. It is the king of the nettles, growing more than 70 cm (24 in) tall, and forms lush, bushy plants that add a woodland feel to their corner of garden. In May and June this particular dead nettle produces pinkish-red flowers.

BLEEDING HEART

Should the sight of this perennial cause any emotion in a gardener's heart, it might well be tears of joy, as both the plant and its flowers look quite magical. The bleeding heart, with its delicate, feathery foliage, produces long, arching stalks with pendants of heart-shaped, rose-red flowers sporting white teardrops on the inside—hence its name.

Though its flowering season is relatively short, the charm of this perennial and its attractively divided leaves makes it a firm favourite with romantically inclined gardeners.

Autumn or winter is the best time to plant bleeding hearts. They look particularly effective when planted as singles, but if you would prefer a whole group of them, leave about 50 cm (18 in) between each plant. This herbaceous perennial is very fond of semi-shade, so it will tolerate north-facing locations. The shade extends the life of the foliage, which would otherwise wilt in the summer. A moist soil with well-rotted compost and good drainage is equally important. It needs no winter protection, even at temperatures as low as –15 °C (32 °F). After approximately three or four years it is a good idea to dig out the plant and divide its roots so that it doesn't become too dense.

GLOBE FLOWER

Some varieties of the European globe flower (*Trollius Europaeus*) may reach as high as 1 metre (3 ft), but most are content with a more modest height. Indeed, some don't get beyond 15 cm (6 in). However, the size of the plant has no impact on the splendour of its buttery yellow blooms, as its radiance is unfettered even when humidity causes the flowers to roll up into tiny balls. These lovely gems were often woven into garlands used to decorate doorways and churches.

In the wild, this flower typically adorns marshes or boggy meadows, often in large groups. It follows that the garden cultivars prefer semi-shady spots with continuously damp soil, which is why they are ideal around ponds or water features, though they are not terribly fussy and will grow well even far from water. At flowering time, between June and August, they will need additional watering and ideally a humus- and nutrient-rich soil. To maintain the condition of the ground where globe flower is planted, it pays to cover the spot in winter. They can be propagated by seed or division.

ORIENTAL POPPY

Finding exactly the right spot for the striking, red oriental poppies, also known as fire poppies, can be a difficult thing to work out. It's not just a matter of considering where the delightfully assertive blooms would look best in the garden, but also what to do when the plant's naturally early demise (or dormancy) occurs in June. A few plants that flower later in the summer should be put next to any oriental poppies to mask the unsightly dried up foliage. This amount of forethought is a small price to pay for the poppy's flamboyant, silky blooms, which stand up to 1 metre (3 ft) high and about 15 cm (6 in) wide. With their black filament tassels, they are unrivalled beauties.

Apart from the most common red flowering types, oriental

poppies do come in other more muted shades, such as the appealing salmon pink.

This perennial should either be planted in October or not until spring. Be careful of the thick roots, which can be quite brittle. The name of the plant conjures up exotic sun-swept lands and its preferred position in the garden is definitely sunny, though it will tolerate semi-shade.

Once it has taken root, it will not wilt when dry, but it does need watering, especially just after planting. No special protection is necessary before winter. A support system installed in spring will help the thin stalks carry their heavy burden of flowers and reach their full height. Cut off any deadheads and you may be rewarded with a second flowering.

SPURGE

There are about 2,000 varieties of the spurge, ranging from a small ground covering plant to the fully-grown African savannah tree, some of which we have already encountered in the rock garden section.

There is much more to be said about one of the types already mentioned by name: the thick, fleshy leaves of the creeping spurge spiral around the stems and heads of the golden yellow bracts (upper leaves). Gardeners appreciate both the plant's foliage and its late spring flowers, as this perennial has the practical habit of beautifying

walls or large rocks. For this reason, the creeping spurge is suitable for tucking into plaster gaps and rock crevices.

The soil can be quite ordinary, but the position should be a sunny one. Creeping spurge requires little care and attention, but trimming the deadheads will encourage further growth. Spurge will survive the winter without assistance.

Less conspicuous but longer-stemmed flowers are borne by the native variety, or so-called Cypress spurge. It gets its name from its tree-like, lean growth pattern.

TENDING
THE GARDEN

PEST CONTROL

Gardeners these days are becoming aware that chemical sprays in the fight against insects, mites, larvae, caterpillars, aphids and other small fry classed as pests should only be used when all biological efforts have failed. This will only be the case very occasionally, and even less frequently in a small garden.

Pest destruction products developed in the lab can be very effective, but you can never limit their effect to the exact area you want to treat.

Like some drugs, none of these chemical pest controls work without side effects, and since many chemicals are difficult or impossible to break down in nature, they can end up damaging the food chain and causing even greater harm than the little creatures they are designed to kill.

Long-term use of the insecticide DDT has taught us a hard lesson. It caused so much collateral damage that it was banned many years ago. Another problem with chemicals, which pharmaceutical manufacturers also struggle with, is the fact that many pest strains have developed resistance to certain poisons over time, or have learnt to avoid the chemical traps. Increasing the amount of pesticide used has had little effect either—in fact, quite the reverse, as the risk of cancer from harmful

The number of ecologically sensible options for pest control is greater than many people think. Some of the simplest methods, apart from picking off pests by hand, are devices like this insect trap which can be hung in fruit trees (right).

146

We have mentioned the role of birds and other useful creatures in keeping unwanted insects in check, but we can take a hand in pest control, too. The simplest method is to inspect your plants and collect any pests by hand. We have also discussed cultivating mixed beds, where plants provide mutual support for each other in the fight against pests. More information on setting up various kinds of pest traps and deterrents is set out in greater detail on the following pages.

Only if all natural methods fail should you resort to "tougher" measures (left).

A brushwood pile is an excellent refuge for useful creatures (below), and a perfect hiding place for insect-eating lizards (bottom).

chemicals in the environment has increased. The latest pest control laws now prohibit the use of many agents once used in the garden.

People have come to realize that it is better to encourage nature to help itself. Desirable organisms and natural enemies of pests are now welcomed, while the natural pest-resistance of edible plants and ornamentals is cultivated with the help of good soil conditioning and maintenance. Horticulture is also cooperating by developing less susceptible, more robust varieties.

The focus is now on achieving an ecological balance between beneficial and harmful garden influences. This can only be accomplished in moderation wherever people are involved, as gardening means manipulating nature in some way to suit our own purposes, which inevitably disturbs the natural balance. Nevertheless, every gardener can do some simple things to work in harmony with nature, such as creating nesting places for birds. The garden songsters are great pest destroyers. In the breeding season, which is also peak time for pests, our feathered friends make short work of caterpillars and larvae.

BREWS AND LIQUID MANURES

The best—and cheapest—safeguard is self-protection. This is certainly true in the garden, which is better able to protect itself from pests if it remains healthy. Perhaps that's why the remedies nature provides are often protective agents and manures in one. Liquid manures and brews keep pests at bay, fight disease and strengthen plants.

So-called liquid manure is made by a fermentation process that works by soaking plants in water for a long time. The optimum ratio is generally ten parts water to one part plants. Don't place the mixture too close to the house, as it develops a strong smell the as it ferments. It will progress better if you place the container in the sun and cover it with gauze, so that nothing falls inside but the air can still circulate. Definitely avoid metal containers; you will have more success with wooden tubs or plastic buckets.

Don't fill them to the brim, as the fermentation process generates foam that could make the mixture overflow. The time it takes varies. The whole process will take at least a week, but sometimes up to three weeks. You will be able to tell when it has finished fermenting when no new foam is produced and the mixture has turned a dark colour. Of course, you'll want to

With a homemade brew of stinging nettle you can do your bit towards ecological pest control in your garden.

keep these mixtures away from pets and children—while not as harsh on the environment as chemical sprays, they most certainly should not be ingested.

Now the liquid is ready to be used, but not before it is diluted by a further one to ten ratio, as it would be too strong for the roots of the plants in its concentrated form. And it is only the roots that you treat, not the leaves, which should be spared any of the mixture wherever possible. To ensure the roots take up the nutrients quickly, try to apply the mixture in light rain, or along with a good dousing from the watering can—or at least in damp conditions.

Which plants are suitable for becoming liquid manures? The stinging nettle is particularly appropriate, as the very substance that makes it so unappealing is equally undesirable to pests. It also helps that these plants grow just about anywhere and are always in good supply. Stinging nettle manure is good for seedlings or planting holes,

as it strengthens the main spur and deters the little critters that like to nibble on roots. A manure that is still being fermented will be very strong, but still tolerated by foliage. This makes it suitable for use in the fight against aphids.

Wormwood and comfrey, dandelion and ferns, onions and garlic are also good sources of liquid manure. Brews on the other hand, i.e. boiled liquids, are better concocted from chamomile, common tansy or field horsetail. To do this, soak the 1:10 mixture (chamomile 1:20) for a day and a night, then boil it for 20 minutes and leave it in the pot with the lid on to cool. Sieve the liquid and after diluting it again use it to water or spray your plants. Field horsetail is good for fungal infections in plants; common tansy combats mildew; while chamomile acts primarily as a plant tonic, encouraging more vigorous growth.

An equally ecological form of pest control is the practice of scattering stone meal (above) over plants.

Spraying roses with a solution of soft soap and denatured spirit is an effective method of controlling aphids (left).

FENCES AND TRAPS

Since word has got around that gardeners with poisonous sprays are not doing themselves any favours, the arsenal of natural defence mechanisms against uninvited guests has grown enormously. It just goes to show how inventive people can be when circumstances force them to seek alternative solutions.

Grease bands (above) are among the preventative pest control methods aimed at specific species. They protect fruit trees in the simplest possible way from harmful insects.

Ingenuity in the fight against garden pests has been aided by the fact that chemical remedies are entirely powerless in some cases. No chemical has yet been found to combat the black vine weevil, for instance — a beetle that eats leaves, while its larvae feed on the rootstock of countless ornamental and edible plants, particularly rhododendrons. This persistent pest can only be removed by the gardener's own intervention — gathering them at night by torchlight, digging out the larvae and burning them by day. You can also buy useful predators that like to attack the larvae and then die once their source of food is extinguished.

Fireblight is another thing resistant to any chemicals. It is a bacterial infection that particularly attacks fruit trees, but hawthorn and rowan trees can also suffer with it. It is spread by birds and insects, but is primarily passed on by infected garden tools. Disinfecting your tools regularly, particularly shears and knives, is the best means of prevention. Once fire blight does strike, however, the only thing for it is to clear away any affected trees and destroy them.

drown. Opponents object on the grounds that some of these slimy pests would never have come in the first place if the beer hadn't lured them in the way a pub attracts drinkers. Maybe some of them think it's a waste of good beer. Anyway, coffee is just as effective, say others, and there have been plenty of plausible reports of good strike rates.

With these remedies it's all a matter of what you believe in, but the following methods will definitely help, even though they will never

Wormwood leaves are a simple and successful means of catching ants on apple trees (left).

Yellow or blue panels coated with sticky paste attract certain pests and work in a similar way to conventional flytraps.

This serves to illustrate how important it is to take preventative action. The more you know about what makes your plants resistant to disease and the more conscientious you are about looking after them, the less likely you are to have major problems. Preventative measures won't eliminate all risks, as pest encroachment cannot be resisted by good garden maintenance alone—it only takes a summer slug invasion to illustrate this point. When this happens the first greedy specimens of the Spanish slug and the common black variety slime their way into our gardens in the spring and new contingents arrive until well into autumn.

There are special slug and snail fences on the market that offer reliable protection for your plants. This won't be necessary in all regions, as there are other proven methods worth trying. Many gardeners swear by beer traps, in which countless snails have been known to

A classic, but still controversial, means of ecological pest control is the beer-filled slug trap.

eliminate the problems completely: Ash, sand and sawdust zones around the most popular edible plants form almost impenetrable barriers. Placing boards in the garden in August will trick snails into laying their eggs underneath. You can easily dispose of them, keeping the pest population down in the following year. Patiently collect snails and slugs and destroy them immediately. Their natural enemies are hedgehogs, toads, lizards, slowworms, shrews, birds and large beetles—the wise gardener will ensure there is plenty of room for these pest predators to thrive.

Methods to kill aphids, mottled umber moths and other insects include placing grease bands around the trunks of fruit trees. The sticky hurdles prevent aphids from harming the branches of Cox orange or early dessert apple trees. A whitefly attack can mean the loss of the whole tree, as affected boughs will often freeze at low temperatures. Whether it helps to remove any sick branches is doubtful, as these white hairy creatures may have long since moved on by the time you discover the damage.

Grease bands also prevent the female of the flightless mottled umber moth from laying her eggs, as the moths are thus unable to reach the buds in the crown of the tree. October is the right time to apply the bands to the trunks.

All kinds of nets are available for garden pest-control use, but some even offer "protection" from useful creatures. Without nets your sweet cherry crop may be gobbled up by blackbirds and starlings, which are otherwise a welcome presence, as they eat large amounts of harmful insects and larvae and feed them to their young. Of course, growing enough for yourself and the birds, or accepting a smaller crop, can solve this problem. Nets or horticultural fleece over vegetable plots will keep real pests at bay, like the so-called vegetable fly. The flies themselves are harmless but their white larvae can cause tremendous damage to your vegetable patch and make big inroads on your crops. A newer form of defence is yellow or blue sticky panels that are hung in branches or on cultivated plants. They are irresistible to certain aphids, black fungus gnats and particularly whiteflies, which are attracted to yellow. Some years you will need plenty of panels, as this pest tends to come out in droves and lay waste to your fuchsias, geraniums, container plants and vegetables. The brightly coloured panels will attract the flies and ensure they come to a sticky end.

This strange-looking object is a readily available trap for plum moths.

Miniature windmills act as a scarecrow to fend off small creatures.

BENEFICIAL INSECTS: LITTLE HELPERS

The circle closes. At the beginning of this chapter we talked about beneficial creatures as natural allies in the fight against pests. The main focus there was on birds. Now it's time to look at the smaller brigade of garden helpers. What they lack in size they make up for in sheer numbers–as long as you give them the opportunity.

Cute looking ladybirds are extremely useful, as they eat plenty of aphids and ensure that a good balance between beneficial and harmful insects is maintained.

Many people are aware that ladybirds like nothing better than to feast on aphids. This is probably due to the high profile of this popular creepy crawly, with its attractive spots and its reputation in many parts as a good luck charm.

However, many other small creatures suffer from misconceptions and widespread prejudices against them, rather than informed insights. Some are feared or considered so ugly that they must be "vermin", yet they are the very creatures that strike the delicate balance in the eating and being eaten equation, which is so important to the health of plants in any small garden.

Let's stay with the ladybird for now, which comes with two or seven black dots on its red wing case. There is even a 14-dot beetle that has lots of yellow spots on its black wing case (this one can also be yellow with black spots). Researchers have recently discovered some of the large American 17-dot version in Europe, with the distinctive heart-shaped pattern on the thorax. Unfortunately this ladybird eats beneficial insects as well, so some fear it may threaten the native varieties.

All these beetles eat aphids—an adult of the two-dot species, for instance, can consume up to 30 aphids each day. But the larvae of these beetles also feed on these most persistent of all garden pests, and in addition devour whitefly and other small scaly insects. Each larva may consume up to 600 aphids by the time they pupate. Nobody would kill the cute, round ladybirds but the larvae are not as safe, since only a very few people are able to recognise them for what they are. Since they're quite small and look like other less desirable larva or crawling bugs, many of these beneficial creatures become the victims of particularly vigilant gardeners.

The persecution suffered by spiders is equally unfortunate. Like ladybird larvae, they don't possess the necessary charisma. On the contrary, they are considered horrible creatures by many people because of their (supposedly) unsightly appearance and eight-legged gangliness, which seems to unleash phobias in some people.

The wonderfully crafted females are skilful web builders (the male's only contribution of note being to ensure the survival of the species) and catch a remarkable number of flying and crawling pests. While there's no need to invite spiders into your living room, you should be very grateful for any that make a home in your garden and on no account destroy their intricate webs that glisten so

A spider mite predator (left) with its prey: it sucks out spider mites and their eggs.

The larva of the aphid midge devouring an aphid (below).

beautifully in the early morning dew. There are no poisonous spiders in Britain to speak of, and even the rare bite of a cross spider makes little more impression than a mosquito bite.

The European or common earwig suffers from similar prejudices. It looks like a mini scorpion and its back leg pincers have given rise to the ridiculous superstition that it creeps inside ears to cause who knows what kind of damage. Unfortunately adults who suffer under this misapprehension tend to pass the myth on to their children, which is why it is so persistent.

Yet the earwig also devours aphids and adds to the competition that makes things so interesting in the garden and anywhere else, for that matter. So if you encounter the creepy crawlies under stones or boards, in casements or in mulch, be thankful that you have them instead of reacting with an "ugh!" An even better response would be to provide the earwigs with a good refuge by hanging dry, upturned flowerpots filled with wood shavings or straw in fruit trees.

The lacewing boxes now available on the market make a good home for the beneficial lacewing, but you could even build one yourself with a little D.I.Y. carpentry skill (right).

Both the beautiful lacewing (greatly enlarged) and its larvae are natural enemies of the aphid (below).

A whole range of other beneficial insects can help you control uninvited guests. The beautiful lacewing, sometimes referred to as the "gold eye", is always in

Although the common earwig (left) is an acknowledged helper, it is often treated as a pest because it occasionally snacks on leaves itself.

Earwigs feel quite at home in these so-called earwig pots: dry, upturned flowerpots filled with straw (left) that are hung up in fruit trees.

hot pursuit of aphids, and their larvae are equally good hunters. They have even earned themselves the nickname "aphid lions". Some shops sell boxes where these winged helpers can base themselves between feeding forays.

And then there is the cabbage aphid parasite that lays its eggs in aphids or caterpillars. Once the larvae hatch they consume the host pest from the inside out. Even some of the creatures normally considered pests can lend a helping hand. Nematodes or parasitic worms are generally a threat to the garden, as many species attack the roots of plants. However, there are also some that feed on root devourers. These beneficial worms are sold in shops. Once they have finished their destructive task, they tend to die for lack of food, which means they help to destroy pests without becoming one in the process.

Beneficial creatures generally make it through the winter as adults while pests survive in egg or larval state. If you use chemical agents in the spring, your beneficial predators will fall victim to them, while the objects of the exercise survive. If you choose not to spray, the pests will hatch but will soon be eaten by the healthy predators that lie in wait for them.

PICTURE CREDITS

MEV, Augsburg: 40 t., 46, 47, 48, 51

all other illustrations:
Silvestris Fotoservice, Kastl